The Open University

Mathematics Foundation Course Unit 12

DIFFERENTIATION I

Prepared by the Mathematics Foundation Course Team

Correspondence Text 12

The Open University Press

Open University courses provide a method of study for independent learners through an integrated teaching system including textual material, radio and television programmes and short residential courses. This text is one of a series that make up the correspondence element of the Mathematics Foundation Course.

The Open University's courses represent a new system of university level education. Much of the teaching material is still in a developmental stage. Courses and course materials are, therefore, kept continually under revision. It is intended to issue regular up-dating notes as and when the need arises, and new editions will be brought out when necessary.

Further information on Open University courses may be obtained from The Admissions Office, The Open University, P.O. Box 48, Bletchley, Buckinghamshire.

The Open University Press
Walton Hall, Bletchley, Bucks.

First published 1971
Copyright © 1971 The Open University

Printed in Great Britain by
J W Arrowsmith Ltd. Bristol 3

SBN 335 01011 3

Contents

Objectives

After working through this unit you should be able to:

(i) explain in your own words why it is necessary to employ a limiting process in forming a derivative;

(ii) define the following terms:
average rate of change,
instantaneous rate of change,
derivative,
derived function,
differentiable,
D, D^2, D^3, etc., where D is the differentiation operator;

(iii) differentiate (using the table of standard forms):
sums of functions,
products of functions,
quotients of functions,
inverse functions,
exponential and logarithmic functions,
trigonometric functions,
composite functions involving any of the above;

(iv) use the method of logarithmic differentiation to obtain derived functions;

(v) determine the gradient of the tangent to a given curve at any given point on the curve;

(vi) determine the velocity and acceleration of a body, given its position as a function of time.

N.B.

Before working through this correspondence text, make sure you have read the general introduction to the mathematics course in the Study Guide, as this explains the philosophy underlying the whole course. You should also be familiar with the section which explains how a text is constructed and the meanings attached to the stars and other symbols in the margin, as this will help you to find your way through the text.

Structural Diagram

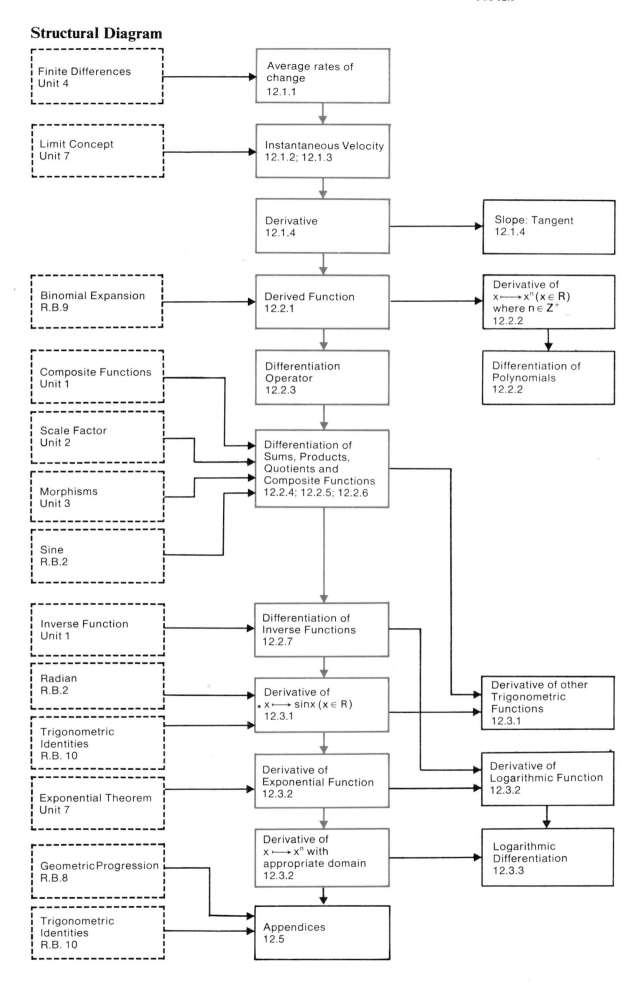

Glossary

Terms which are defined in this glossary are printed in CAPITALS.

ACCELERATION	ACCELERATION is the rate of change of VELOCITY; it is the DERIVATIVE of the function:	45

$$\text{time} \longmapsto \text{velocity.}$$

AVERAGE RATE OF CHANGE	The AVERAGE RATE OF CHANGE of the image of a function f over an interval $[x_1, x_2]$ in its domain is	4

$$\frac{f(x_2) - f(x_1)}{x_2 - x_1}.$$

AVERAGE VELOCITY	The AVERAGE VELOCITY over the time interval $[t_1, t_2]$ is	1, 3

$$\frac{\text{distance travelled in } [t_1, t_2]}{\text{duration of } [t_1, t_2]}.$$

CHAIN RULE, COMPOSITE FUNCTION RULE	The COMPOSITE FUNCTION RULE (also called the CHAIN RULE or FUNCTION OF A FUNCTION RULE) states:	33

$$(f \circ g)' = (f' \circ g) \times g'$$

where f and g are DIFFERENTIABLE functions.

DERIVATIVE	The DERIVATIVE of a function f at t is	11

$$\lim_{h \to 0} \frac{f(t + h) - f(t)}{h}.$$

DERIVED FUNCTION	The DERIVED FUNCTION of a function f is	17

$$f': x \longmapsto \text{DERIVATIVE of } f \text{ at } x.$$

The domain of f' is the subset of the domain of f consisting of elements at which f is DIFFERENTIABLE.

DIFFERENTIABLE	A function is said to be DIFFERENTIABLE at those points of its domain at which the DERIVATIVE exists. If no points of the domain are mentioned, we mean that the function is differentiable at all points of its domain.	17
DIFFERENTIATE	To DIFFERENTIATE a function is to find its DERIVED FUNCTION.	17
DIFFERENTIATION OPERATOR	The operator $D: f \longmapsto f'$ ($f \in$ set of real functions) is called the DIFFERENTIATION OPERATOR.	23
FUNCTION OF A FUNCTION RULE	See COMPOSITE FUNCTION RULE.	
INSTANTANEOUS RATE OF CHANGE	The INSTANTANEOUS RATE OF CHANGE of a function, f, at the element x in its domain is $f'(x)$.	11
INSTANTANEOUS VELOCITY	The INSTANTANEOUS VELOCITY of an object at time t is $\lim_{h \to 0}$ (average velocity over $[t, t + h]$)	9
INVERSE FUNCTION RULE	The INVERSE FUNCTION RULE states: if f is a one-one function with inverse g, then	41

$$g' = \frac{1}{f' \circ g}$$

LOGARITHMIC DIFFERENTIATION	LOGARITHMIC DIFFERENTIATION is a method of DIFFERENTIATING a product of functions, fgh say, by writing the product in the form: $$fgh = \exp(\ln f + \ln g + \ln h)$$ or $$\ln(fgh) = \ln f + \ln g + \ln h,$$ before differentiating. This gives: $$\frac{(fgh)'}{(fgh)} = \frac{f'}{f} + \frac{g'}{g} + \frac{h'}{h}.$$	49
MAGNIFICATION	The MAGNIFICATION (SCALE FACTOR) of an object is: $$\frac{\text{size of image}}{\text{size of original}}.$$	31
PRODUCT RULE	The PRODUCT RULE states: $$(fg)' = f'g + g'f$$ where f and g are DIFFERENTIABLE functions. The domain of $(fg)'$ is the intersection of the domains of f' and g'.	29
QUOTIENT RULE	The QUOTIENT RULE states: $$\left(\frac{f}{g}\right)' = \frac{f'g - g'f}{g^2}$$ where f and g are DIFFERENTIABLE functions. The domain of $\left(\dfrac{f}{g}\right)'$ is the subset of the intersection of the domains of f' and g' consisting of all those elements, x, at which $g(x) \neq 0$.	37
RATIONAL FUNCTION	A RATIONAL FUNCTION is a quotient of polynomial functions (see *Unit 1*).	43
REAL FUNCTION	A REAL FUNCTION is a function whose domain and codomain are subsets of R.	23
SECOND DERIVED FUNCTION	The SECOND DERIVED FUNCTION of a function f is the DERIVED FUNCTION of the derived function of f; that is: $f'' : x \longmapsto$ DERIVATIVE of f' at x. The domain of f'' is the subset of the domain of f' consisting of elements at which f' is DIFFERENTIABLE.	24
SIMPLE HARMONIC MOTION	SIMPLE HARMONIC MOTION is an oscillatory motion in which the ACCELERATION at time t is proportional to the displacement at time t. The displacement, x, is of the form: $$x = x_0 + a \sin b(t - t_0),$$ where a and b are constants and t_0, x_0 are the initial time and the initial displacement respectively.	45
SLOPE OF TANGENT	The SLOPE OF THE TANGENT (if it exists) at x to a curve specified by the equation $y = f(x)$ is $f'(x)$.	12
STANDARD FORMS	STANDARD FORMS are expressions for DERIVED FUNCTIONS of polynomial, rational, trigonometric, exponential and logarithmic functions.	43
TANGENT	The TANGENT (if it exists) at x to the curve specified by the equation $y = f(x)$ is the straight line which touches the curve at $(x, f(x))$.	12
VELOCITY	See AVERAGE VELOCITY and INSTANTANEOUS VELOCITY.	

Notation

The symbols are presented in the order in which they appear in the text.

Bibliography

T. M. Apostol, *Calculus*, Vol. I (Blaisdell 1967).
This is an extremely well written book suitable for students who need a rigorous discussion of differentiation and the associated techniques. It also covers many topics of fundamental importance to Foundation Course students and others.

M. Bruckheimer, *et al.*, *Mathematics for Technology* (Chatto and Windus 1968).
This book uses a "new style" approach to mathematics which makes interesting and pleasant reading. The student is warned to work through all the exercises (solutions are given), otherwise he may miss the important points. The notation is very similar to that used in our Foundation Course.

M. Spivâk, *Calculus* (Benjamin 1967).
This gives a good treatment of calculus and introduction to analysis. The book contains very good diagrams and is easy to read.

S. K. Stein, *Calculus for the Natural and Social Sciences* (McGraw-Hill 1968).
This is a pleasantly written and very readable book which has many helpful diagrams and illustrations.

J. C. Burkill, *A First Course in Mathematical Analysis* (Cambridge University Press 1962).
This gives a rigorous treatment of differential calculus (Chapter 4); it contains very few diagrams and not many illustrations. It is recommended to students who intend to specialize in Mathematics.

12.0 INTRODUCTION

In this unit we shall be concerned with change, and, in particular, the rate at which things change.

Everything in the physical world about us is changing, sometimes rapidly, sometimes very slowly. We know, for example, that plants are growing; so their sizes are changing, albeit very slowly. We know too that an insect's wings move as it flies, even though they usually beat so rapidly that it is impossible for us to follow the movement with our eyes. An intermediate example is the movement of a motor car. Here it is the position of the car that is changing, and we have an instrument in the car which measures the rate of change of position, namely the speedometer.

The general aim of this unit is to set up a mathematical scheme for describing and measuring rates of change. Because everybody has some familiarity with velocity and acceleration, we have chosen motion as our starting point. The ideas we shall develop are, however, of great generality. They are used not only in kinematics (the study of velocities and accelerations) but also in studying many other types of rate of change, such as the rate of population growth; the rate at which the boiling point of water changes with height on a mountain; the rate at which the temperature in a room decreases with distance from a radiator, and so on. In the first section we are mainly concerned with the mathematical description of these rates of change, that is, with the concept of the derivative of a function. In the second and third sections we establish some rules for finding derivatives.

As we remarked in *Unit 9*, our notation for the calculus is different from the classical notation which is used in most textbooks; our notation is consistent with our basic approach to mathematics through the concept of a function. Once you have mastered the basic principles, there is no objection to your using the traditional Leibniz notation which is discussed in Appendix I on page 56.

Leibniz   (Mansell)
(1646–1716)

12.1 RATES OF CHANGE

12.1.1 Average Rates of Change

We have already discussed the concept of average velocity in *Unit 7, Sequences and Limits I*. The purpose of this sub-section is simply to remind you how average velocity is defined, and to consider some of the consequences of the definition.

To illustrate the idea of average velocity, suppose you made a car journey from London to Edinburgh and recorded the total distance covered at hourly intervals. The recorded data might be given in the following table:

Table I

Time (h)	Distance (km)
0	0
1	15
2	110
3	200
4	240
5	300
6	390
7	480
8	570
9	600

The table shows that at time 0 the distance travelled is 0, where time 0 is the time at which the journey begins. After one hour the car has covered 15 km. After two hours it has covered 110 km, i.e. in the second hour it has covered 95 km. In the third hour it has covered 90 km, but in the fourth and fifth hours it has only covered 40 and 60 km respectively—perhaps you stopped for lunch. Then the car covered 90 km in each of the sixth, seventh and eighth hours of the journey. In the ninth hour it only covered 30 km; perhaps the traffic was heavy near Edinburgh.

In discussing your trip to Edinburgh with a friend who has made a similar long journey you might wish to compare your average velocity with his. To calculate it you would divide the distance travelled by the time:*

$$\text{average velocity} = \frac{\text{distance travelled}}{\text{time}}$$

$$= \frac{600\,\text{km}}{9\,\text{h}}$$

$$= 66.7\,\text{km/h}.$$

Alternatively, you might wish to compare your average velocities over different parts of the journey; for example:

$$\text{average velocity over first 3 hours} = \frac{\text{distance travelled}}{\text{time}}$$

$$= \frac{200\,\text{km}}{3\,\text{h}}$$

$$= 66.7\,\text{km/h}$$

---

* Velocity means speed in a known direction. Here we assume that the road is straight so that only two directions of motion are possible; away from London and towards it. We distinguish them by giving the velocity a positive sign for motion away from London, and a negative sign for motion towards it.

$$\text{average velocity over last 3 hours} = \frac{600\,\text{km} - 390\,\text{km}}{9\,\text{h} - 6\,\text{h}}$$

$$= \frac{210}{3}\,\text{km/h}$$

$$= 70\,\text{km/h}.$$

In each case the method of calculation is an application of the formula given in the Introduction to *Unit 7, Sequences and Limits I*: average velocity over time interval $[t_1, t_2]$ is

$$\frac{\text{distance travelled in } [t_1, t_2]}{\text{duration of } [t_1, t_2]} = \frac{x_2 - x_1}{t_2 - t_1} \qquad \text{Equation (1)}$$

where x_1 and x_2 are the distances from London at the times t_1 and t_2 respectively. The essential restriction on t_1 and t_2 (apart from the obvious one that they must be among the instants for which the distances of the car from London are given) is that they must be different; that is, $t_2 > t_1$, for if $t_2 = t_1$, then the fraction in Equation (1) has denominator zero, and fractions with zero denominator have no meaning. We shall return to this important point in section 12.1.2.

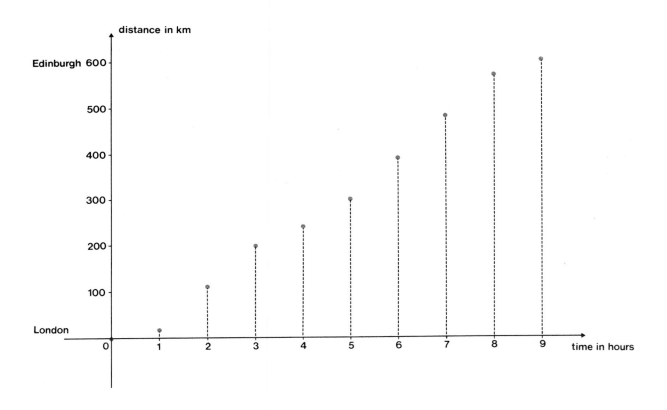

Average velocities have a very convenient representation in terms of pictorial graphs. The figure below shows how we can use the graph to calculate the average velocity over the time interval [6, 9]. In the right-angled triangle ABC, the side AB corresponds to a time, 3 hours, and BC corresponds to a distance, $(600 - 390)\,\text{km} = 210\,\text{km}$. The magnitude of the average velocity over [6, 9] is $\frac{210}{3}$ which is the slope of AC (i.e. $\tan CAB$).

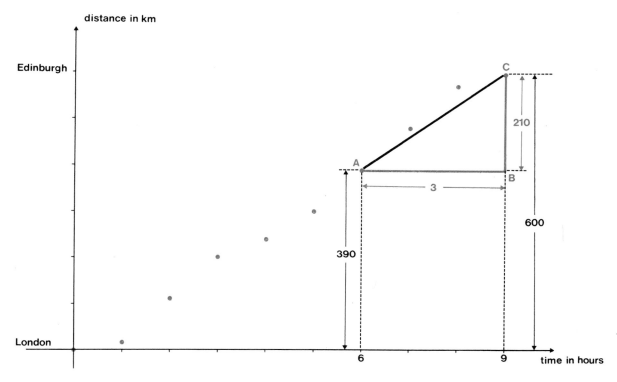

Similarly, the magnitude of the average velocity over any time interval, $[t_1, t_2]$, as given by Equation (1), is the slope of the straight line joining the two points on the pictorial graph corresponding to t_1 and t_2; the unit of the average velocity is km/h.

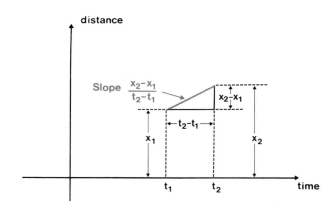

The concept which underlies average velocity can be generalized to many other situations, if we first pick out its essential feature with the help of the concept of a function. In the example of the car journey, the relevant function is the one tabulated in Table I:

f:(time since start) $\longmapsto$ (distance travelled).

In terms of this function, the formula for average velocity is:

$$\text{average velocity over the interval } [t_1, t_2] = \frac{f(t_2) - f(t_1)}{t_2 - t_1}$$

Equation (2)

3

Expressions of the type used in Equation (2) can be useful for many other situations involving rates of change. For example, $f(t)$ may represent the quantity of water in a reservoir at time t. In this case, the expression on the right of Equation (2) has the interpretation

$$\frac{f(t_2) - f(t_1)}{t_2 - t_1} = \frac{\text{change in quantity of water in reservoir during } [t_1, t_2]}{\text{duration of } [t_1, t_2]}.$$

That is, it gives the average rate at which the quantity of water in the reservoir changes during $[t_1, t_2]$. As another example, f might be the function:

$$f : (\text{depth below sea level}) \longmapsto (\text{hydrostatic pressure})$$

(at some particular time and place). In this case, if d_1 and d_2 are two depths,

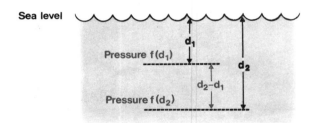

then

$$\frac{f(d_2) - f(d_1)}{d_2 - d_1} = \frac{\text{corresponding change in pressure}}{\text{change in depth}}$$

$$= \text{average rate of change of pressure with depth.}$$

The value of this fraction is roughly 0.1 atmosphere per metre. An aquanaut can use this value to deduce his depth changes from measured changes in pressure.

In general, if f is any real function (i.e. a function whose domain and codomain are subsets of R), we define:

Average rate of change of $f(t)$ over the interval $[t_1, t_2]$ is

$$\frac{f(t_2) - f(t_1)}{t_2 - t_1}.$$

Definition 1
* *

Exercise 1

Exercise 1
(3 minutes)

Add a third column to Table I (reproduced below), showing the first differences of the tabulated values of the function f, with domain $[0, 9]$, defined by:

$$f : (\text{time since start}) \longmapsto (\text{distance travelled}).$$

(See *Unit 4, Finite Differences* for the definition of first differences, and also for the notation Δ_h.)

4

Time (h)	Distance (km)	First Difference (km)
0	0	
1	15	
2	110	
3	200	
4	240	
5	300	
6	390	
7	480	
8	570	
9	600	

(i) What is the interpretation of the numbers in the third column in terms of average velocity?

(ii) How is the function $\Delta_1 f$ connected with average velocity?

(iii) If we define $\frac{1}{h}\Delta_h f$ to be the function:

$$t \longmapsto \frac{1}{h}\{f(t+h) - f(t)\}\,(t \in [0, 9-h]), \text{ where } 0 < h < 9,$$

how is this function connected with average velocity? ∎

12.1.2 The Need for Instantaneous Velocities

12.1.2

Discussion

The average velocities obtainable from the data given in the last section give only a very crude indication of the speeds at which the car travels during the journey. For example, the car took one hour to cover the first 15 kilometres. Was this a relatively steady 15 km/h or did the car travel at 30 km/h for roughly half the time and spend most of the other half standing in traffic jams?

There is no way of answering this question from the data given in Table I of the preceding section. To answer it we would need more detailed information, such as a table showing the total distance after each minute of the journey, instead of each hour. Here is part of a hypothetical table of this kind for the London–Edinburgh journey:

Time (min)	Distance (km)
0	0
1	0.1
2	0.35
3	0.6
4	0.6
5	0.6
6	0.6
…	…
60	15.0
…	…

It looks as though there was a traffic jam 0.6 km from the starting point. From such a table we can calculate average velocities just as before; for example, the average velocity during the third minute was 0.25 km/min,

(continued on page 6)

Time (h)	Distance (km)	First Difference (km)
0	0	
		15
1	15	
		95
2	110	
		90
3	200	
		40
4	240	
		60
5	300	
		90
6	390	
		90
7	480	
		90
8	570	
		30
9	600	

(i) The numbers in the third column are the average velocities (in km/h) during the hour in question: 15 km/h during the first hour, 95 km/h during the second hour, etc. (This is because the intervals are each of length one hour. If they were each of length two hours, for instance, we would have to divide the first differences by two to get average velocities.)

(ii) $\Delta_1 f(t)$ is the average velocity during the time interval $[t, t + 1]$. Again, it is the subscript 1 that allows us to identify $\Delta_1 f(t)$ with average velocity. If we change the interval h, then the average velocity becomes $\frac{1}{h} \Delta_h f(t)$, *not* just $\Delta_h f(t)$. (Notice that in this case Δ_1 is defined for $[0, 8]$ only.)

(iii) $\frac{1}{h} \Delta_h f(t)$ is the average velocity during the time interval $[t, t + h]$. ∎

(*continued from page 5*)

that is, 15 km/h. But once again, such average velocities give only a rough idea of the speed of the car as measured by the speedometer. Was the speed during this third minute a steady 15 km/h, or did the driver accelerate to a much higher speed during the first part and then brake sharply? The table above enables us to locate the traffic jams (assuming that they cause the stationary periods) but it gives very little information about how the driver used his brakes, for instance.

To give information about driving habits, the distance function would need to be tabulated with an even smaller time spacing; probably a table showing the distance travelled after every second of the journey would be adequate to provide this type of information. Here is a small part of such a hypothetical table:

Time (s)	Distance (m)
...	...
150	570
151	585
152	595
153	600
...	...

The average velocity during the one-second interval [150, 151] is 15 m/s (54 km/h); during the next interval it is only 10 m/s, and in the following interval it is 5 m/s, indicating that the driver braked sharply (or had a collision).

In *Unit 7, Sequences and Limits I*, we pointed out that if the occupants of the car had been unfortunately involved in a collision, then even the average velocity over the last second before impact would not be of direct interest to them. If the driver were braking sharply during the last second, the actual impact would occur at a speed of several kilometres per hour less than the average speed during the last second, and these few kilometres per hour could make a vital difference to the outcome. Clearly then, there are some purposes for which even a one-second time interval is too long for the computation of a meaningful average velocity over that interval.

It appears from this discussion that to answer any *particular* question involving velocities (Was the car involved in an accident? Was the driver heavy on his brakes? Did the driver accelerate rapidly?), we can, in theory, always find a time interval short enough for average velocities over that interval to be useful in discussing the question. It would obviously be desirable to have a definition of velocity that could be guaranteed in advance to satisfy *all* the demands that might be made on it, instead of possibly having to be adjusted after some new demand became known. That is, we would like to contract to zero the duration of the time interval used in defining velocity, making it *not the average velocity over an interval*, but an *instantaneous velocity*.

A first attempt at such a definition might be to use a time interval of zero duration in the formula for average velocity. Things are not that easy, however. The average velocity over the time interval $[t_1, t_2]$, which we shall in future denote by $w(t_1, t_2)$, was defined in Equation 12.1.1.2 by:

$$w(t_1, t_2) = \frac{f(t_2) - f(t_1)}{t_2 - t_1}$$

where f is the function:

$$f : (\text{time since starting}) \longmapsto (\text{distance travelled}).$$

If we try to use a time interval of zero duration, then we have $t_1 = t_2$ and $f(t_1) = f(t_2)$, so that the fraction on the right-hand side of the equation turns into the expression $\frac{0}{0}$, which is meaningless, since division by zero is not defined.

Exercise 1

What is the fallacy in the following argument?

Exercise 1
(2 minutes)

Let

$$x = 1 \text{ and } y = 1,$$

so that

$$x = y.$$

Then

$$x^2 - y^2 = xy - y^2$$

i.e.

$$(x - y)(x + y) = (x - y)y.$$

So

$$(x + y) = y \quad \text{(after cancelling by the factor } (x - y))$$

i.e.

$$2 = 1 \quad \text{(since } x = 1 \text{ and } y = 1). \quad \blacksquare$$

Solution 1

Cancelling a factor in an equation is the same as dividing throughout by the factor, and is not permissible when that factor is equal to zero. For example, $3 \times 0 = 2 \times 0$, but $3 \neq 2$. Thus, the correct deduction to make from the equation

$$(x - y)(x + y) = (x - y)y$$

is:

$$x + y = y, \text{ if } x - y \neq 0;$$

but in this case

$$x - y = 1 - 1 = 0,$$

so that the deduction $x + y = y$ cannot be made.   ∎

12.1.3   The Definition of Instantaneous Velocity

In the previous section, using average velocities over shorter and shorter
time intervals, we obtained expressions for average velocities which became increasingly satisfactory as the time intervals decreased, in the sense
that they gave us more and more information. We could regard these
successive average velocities over smaller and smaller intervals as successive approximations to the velocity *at a particular instant*. Successive
approximation procedures were considered in *Unit 7, Sequences and
Limits I*, and we saw there how to define a number called the limit of a
real function. In the present case the approximation depends on the
duration of the time interval $[t_1, t_2]$. If we denote the duration $t_2 - t_1$ by h,
then $t_2 = t_1 + h$, and we can define the function g by:

$$g : h \longmapsto w(t_1, t_1 + h) = \frac{f(t_1 + h) - f(t_1)}{h} \quad (h \in \text{subset of } R^+)$$ **Equation (1)**

We are interested in the limit of g near 0, which we shall define to be the
instantaneous velocity at t_1. Similarly, the instantaneous velocity at t_2
can be defined by the limit near 0 of the function:

$$g : h \longmapsto w(t_2 - h, t_2) = \frac{f(t_2) - f(t_2 - h)}{h} \quad (h \in \text{subset of } R^+).$$ **Equation (2)**

To see how this limit can be used to avoid the $\dfrac{0}{0}$ difficulty, try the following

exercise.

Exercise 1

Galileo is (apocryphally) said to have tested the law of gravity by dropping
objects of differing weights from the Leaning Tower of Pisa; we shall
consider a similar experiment. Assuming that after the object has fallen for
t seconds it has fallen exactly $5t^2$ metres, and that it takes exactly 3 seconds
to reach the ground, find the average velocity

  (i) over the last second of fall;
 (ii) over the last tenth of a second;
(iii) over the last hundredth of a second.

What is the instantaneous velocity at the moment of striking the ground?
Can you find a formula for this?   ∎

We can rewrite the definition of average velocity in Equation (2) in the following way:

$$g : h \longmapsto \frac{f(t_2 - h) - f(t_2)}{-h} \quad (h \in \text{subset of } R^+).$$

If we now put $h = -k$, this becomes:

$$g : k \longmapsto \frac{f(t_2 + k) - f(t_2)}{k} \quad \begin{array}{l} (k \in \text{subset of } R^-, \text{ the set of all} \\ \text{negative real numbers}), \end{array}$$

and we see that this has the same form as Equation (1), except that the domain consists of negative numbers instead of positive numbers. So if we consider the function:

$$g : h \longmapsto w(t, t + h) \quad (h \in \text{subset of } R, h \neq 0),$$

then its images give the average velocity over a time interval of length h, beginning or ending at time t, depending on whether h is positive or negative. Although 0 does not belong to the domain of this function, the function can have a limit near 0.

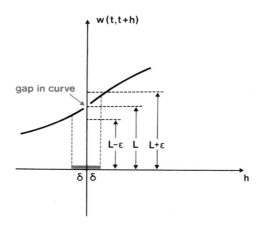

In *Unit 7, Sequences and Limits I*, we defined the limit to be the number, L, (if it exists) such that for each positive number ε, however small, there is a positive number δ such that the image of the set $\{h : -\delta < h < \delta$ and $h \neq 0\}$ is a subset of $[L - \varepsilon, L + \varepsilon]$. The value of this limit is called the instantaneous velocity at time t. If we write $v(t)$ for the instantaneous velocity at time t, this definition takes the form

$$v(t) = \lim_{h \to 0} \frac{f(t + h) - f(t)}{h}$$

$$= \lim_{h \to 0} \left[\frac{1}{h} \Delta_h f(t) \right].$$

Exercise 2

Find the instantaneous velocity at time t of a car which moves in such a way that its distance from some fixed point on the road it travels is at^3 where a is some positive number. ■

Solution 1

The average velocity over the last h seconds of fall is, for $h > 0$,

$$w(3 - h, 3) = \frac{\text{distance travelled in } [3 - h, 3]}{\text{duration of } [3 - h, 3]}$$

$$= \frac{5 \times 3^2 - 5 \times (3 - h)^2}{h}$$

$$= \frac{45 - 5 \times (9 - 6h + h^2)}{h}$$

$$= \frac{30h - 5h^2}{h}$$

$$= 30 - 5h.$$

(This last line can only be obtained from the previous one if we assume $h \neq 0$, since we cannot divide by zero.) So the function we are interested in is:

$$g : h \longmapsto 30 - 5h \qquad (h \in R : 0 < h \leqslant 3).$$

The average velocity over the last second ($h = 1$) is

$$w(2, 3) = 30 - 5 = 25 \text{ m/s}.$$

The average velocity over the last $\frac{1}{10}$ second ($h = 0.1$) is

$$w(2.9, 3) = 30 - 0.5 = 29.5 \text{ m/s}.$$

The average velocity over the last $\frac{1}{100}$ second ($h = 0.01$) is

$$w(2.99, 3) = 30 - 0.05 = 29.95 \text{ m/s}.$$

Taking the limit of g near 0 gives the instantaneous velocity at 3 seconds as

$$\lim_{h \to 0^+}{}^* (30 - 5h) = 30 \text{ m/s}.$$

Notice that this is not the same as $g(0)$, because $g(0)$ does not exist. Of necessity the domain of g does not include 0; the simple expression $30 - 5h$ arises from $\dfrac{30h - 5h^2}{h}$, and the latter expression becomes meaningless if we set $h = 0$. ■

Solution 2

The position of the car at time t is given by the function

$$f : t \longmapsto at^3 \quad (t \in R_0^+, \text{ the set of all non-negative real numbers}).$$

For any t in R_0^+, the average velocity of the car over a time-interval $[t, t + h]$, $h > 0$, is given by:

$$w(t, t + h) = \frac{a(t + h)^3 - at^3}{h}$$

$$= \frac{a(t^3 + 3t^2 h + 3th^2 + h^3) - at^3}{h}$$

$$= 3at^2 + (3ath + ah^2) \quad (h \in R, h > 0)$$

The velocity at time t is then given by

$$v(t) = \lim_{h \to 0} w(t, t + h).$$

It should be intuitively clear that $v(t) = 3at^2$ ($t \in R_0^+$), since the terms $3ath$ and ah^2 tend to zero as h tends to zero. ■

* We use the notation $\lim_{h \to 0^+}$, rather than $\lim_{h \to 0}$, because here we have a "one-sided limit"; that is, h is essentially positive and so h can only tend to 0 via positive values.

12.1.4 The Derivative

Just as the idea of average velocity can be generalized to give a definition of average rate of change for any function, so the idea of an instantaneous velocity can also be generalized to give a definition of rate of change of a real function having no direct connection with kinematics. As in the discussion of average rates of change, all that we have to do is to apply the same formula as in the definition of instantaneous velocity, and call the analogue of instantaneous velocity the (instantaneous) rate of change. That is to say, if f is any real function, we can define the (instantaneous) rate of change of $f(x)$ at the element x in the domain of f, to be the number

$$\lim_{h \to 0} \frac{\Delta_h f(x)}{h}$$

provided that this limit exists. This rate of change at x is usually called the derivative of f at x and it is denoted by $f'(x)$. Thus the velocity of a car t seconds after the start of its journey is equal to the derivative at t of the function (numbers of seconds since starting) $\longmapsto$ (distance since starting).

There are other notations for the derivative: in the most important of them, the Leibniz notation, we write $\dfrac{df(x)}{dx}$ in place of $f'(x)$. This notation is discussed in Appendix I, but familiarity with it is not essential to the Foundation Course.

Like the average rate of change, the instantaneous rate of change, or derivative, has a very useful interpretation in terms of a pictorial graph of the function. We have already seen that the average rate of change of $f(t)$ over an interval $[t_1, t_1 + h]$ equals the slope of the straight line joining the points on the graph corresponding to t_1 and $t_1 + h$.

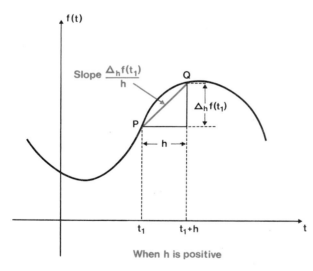

When h is positive

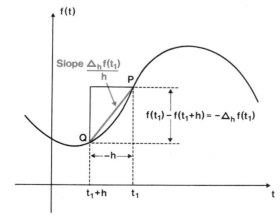

When h is negative

To obtain the derivative at t_1, we let the magnitude of h get smaller and smaller. In the above figures the point denoted by Q then slides (like a bead) along the curve towards the point P which remains fixed. Corresponding to the first diagram, three successive positions for Q are shown below, labelled Q_1, Q_2, Q_3. (We have spaced the points generously round the curve, so that the figure is clear.) The corresponding positions for the

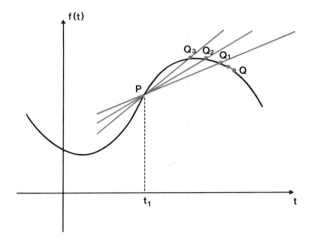

straight line PQ are also shown. As Q approaches P, the line rotates about P, and approaches a limiting position which we define to be the tangent to the curve at P. It follows that when h is very small, the slope of the line PQ is very close to the slope of the tangent at P, and consequently that the limit of the slope of the line PQ near P is equal to the slope of the tangent at P.

Definition 2
* *

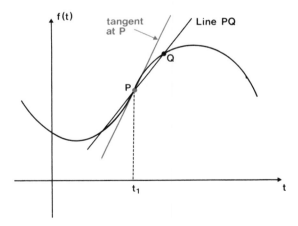

In symbols, using Definition 1, we have: (slope of tangent to graph at P) = (derivative of function at t_1)

The geometrical interpretation of the derivative is very useful, not only in geometry. We shall use it frequently when discussing applications of the derivative; for example, when obtaining approximations to real functions (*Unit 14, Sequences and Limits II*) and when finding the maximum and minimum values of the images of real functions (*Unit 15, Differentiation II*).

There are functions whose graphs do not have tangents at every point. For example, the graph of the function

$$f : x \longmapsto |x| \quad (x \in R)$$

does not have a tangent at $(0, 0)$.

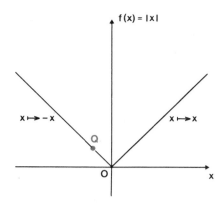

You can see this by considering the slope of the line OQ as Q approaches the origin, O, where Q is a point on the graph. Consider first the case in which Q is a point on the graph of the function $x \longmapsto -x$, and then that when Q is a point on the graph of the function $x \longmapsto x$. The slopes of the lines are respectively -1 and $+1$; the tangent at $(0, 0)$ does not exist. We have

$$\lim_{h \to 0} \frac{\Delta_h f(x)}{h} = \begin{array}{l} +1 \text{ if } x > 0 \\ -1 \text{ if } x < 0 \end{array} \text{ but } \lim_{h \to 0} \frac{\Delta_h f(0)}{h} \text{ does not exist.}$$

We say that the derivative of f at 0 does not exist.

The illustration below shows the graph of another function which has a tangent at each point, except at $(t_1, f(t_1))$. Again, the derivative of the function at t_1 does not exist.

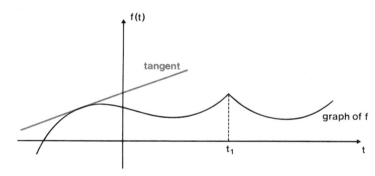

Exercise 1

Which of the following statements are true?

(i) The tangent to a curve at P cannot cross the curve at P.   TRUE/FALSE

(ii) The angle between the tangent to a curve at P and the horizontal axis is the limit, as Q approaches P along the curve, of the angle between the line PQ and this axis.   TRUE/FALSE

(iii) The tangent to a curve at P may be defined as the straight line that meets the curve only at P.   TRUE/FALSE

(iv) If f is continuous at every element in its domain there is a tangent at every point on its graph.   TRUE/FALSE
(See *Unit 7, Sequences and Limits I* for the definition of continuity.)
■

Exercise 2

Show that the derivative of a constant function at any element in its domain is 0.
■

Solution 1 **Solution 1**

(i) FALSE. Consider, for instance, our example of a car whose position is described by

$$f: t \longmapsto at^3 \quad (t \in R_0^+).$$

We found that

$$f'(t) = 3at^2 \quad (t \in R_0^+).$$

Similarly, for the function

$$g: t \longmapsto at^3 \ (t \in R)$$

we can show that

$$g'(t) = 3at^2 \quad (t \in R).$$

The derivative of g at 0 is therefore zero, so the tangent at this point is the t-axis, which crosses the curve specified by $y = g(x)$ at $(0, 0)$.

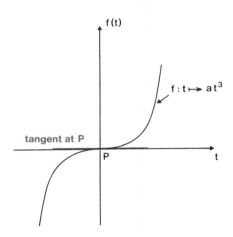

(ii) TRUE, whenever the tangent at P exists.
(iii) FALSE. Consider the following diagram:

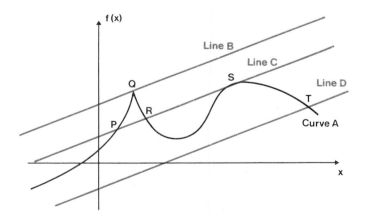

Line B meets the curve A only at Q, but the tangent to the curve at Q does not exist. Line C meets the curve A at P, R and S and is a tangent to the curve at S. Line D meets the curve A at T only, but it is not the tangent to the curve at T.
(iv) FALSE. Consider the modulus function again:

$$f: x \longmapsto |x| \quad (x \in R).$$

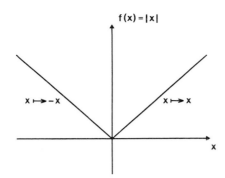

This function is continuous at every element in its domain, and in particular at the origin, O. But

$$\frac{\Delta_h f(0)}{h} = \frac{f(0 + h) - f(0)}{h} = \begin{cases} 1, \text{ if } h > 0 \\ -1, \text{ if } h < 0 \end{cases}$$

so there is no number L for which

$$\lim_{h \to 0} \frac{\Delta_h f(0)}{h} = L.$$

Solution 2   **Solution 2**

Let $f: x \longmapsto a \, (x \in R)$ where a is any real number. Then, for all $x \in R$ and all non-zero $h \in R$, we have:

$$\frac{\Delta_h f(x)}{h} = \frac{f(x + h) - f(x)}{h}$$

$$= \frac{a - a}{h}$$

$$= 0.$$

Thus,

$$f'(x) = \lim_{h \to 0} 0$$

$$= 0.$$

Exercise 3   **Exercise 3**
                                                                      (3 minutes)
If f is defined by

$$f(t) = 5t^2 \qquad (t \in R),$$

find $f'(t)$. (You have solved a similar problem in Exercise 12.1.3.2)

Exercise 4   **Exercise 2**
                                                                      (2 minutes)
Sketch the graph of

$$f: t \longmapsto t^2 \qquad (t \in R).$$

Find $f'(t)$ and evaluate

$$f'(-3), f'(0) \text{ and } f'(2).$$

What can you deduce about the slopes of the tangents to the graph of f at $-3, 0$ and 2?

Sketch these tangents on your graph.

Solution 3

For all $t \in R$, and all non-zero $h \in R$, we have:

$$\frac{\Delta_h f(t)}{h} = \frac{f(t + h) - f(t)}{h}$$

$$= \frac{5(t + h)^2 - 5t^2}{h}$$

$$= 10t + 5h$$

Thus

$$f'(t) = \lim_{h \to 0} (10t + 5h)$$

$$= 10t. \qquad \blacksquare$$

Solution 4

Again, for all $t \in R$ and all non-zero $h \in R$, we have:

$$\frac{\Delta_h f(t)}{h} = \frac{f(t + h) - f(t)}{h}$$

$$= \frac{(t + h)^2 - t^2}{h}$$

$$= 2t + h.$$

Thus,

$$f'(t) = \lim_{h \to 0} (2t + h)$$

$$= 2t.$$

In particular,

$$f'(-3) = -6,$$

$$f'(0) = 0,$$

$$f'(2) = 4;$$

so the slope of the tangent of the graph is negative at -3, zero at 0 and positive at 2.

Your graph should look something like this:

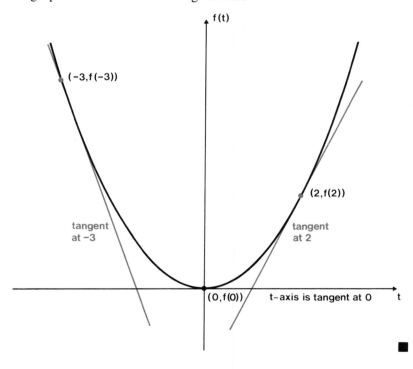

12.2 THE RULES OF DIFFERENTIATION

12.2.0 Introduction

We have already indicated the wide range of applications of the concept of derivative which we defined in the preceding section. To make full use of this concept we need to look at some of the properties of the derivative. The first fruits of this study will be a set of rules which will enable us to calculate derivatives of functions quickly and easily, without having to go back to the definition every time.

12.2.1 The Derived Function

We start with the definition of the derivative of a real function, f, at x:

$$f'(x) = \lim_{h \to 0} \frac{\Delta_h f(x)}{h} = \lim_{h \to 0} \frac{f(x + h) - f(x)}{h}.$$

The derivative is a number; however, since this number depends on the value of x, we can use the notion of derivative to define a function. This function maps x to the value of the derivative of f at x. In fact, by our notation $f'(x)$ we have already implicitly recognized the existence of this function. This new function f' is called the derived function of f, and in finding it we are said to differentiate the function f.

The domain of the derived function will be taken to comprise all the values of x for which $f'(x)$ exists. Since Definition 1 involves f, the domain of the derived function must be a subset of the domain of f. In some cases the two domains may be the same; in others, the domain of f' may be a proper subset of that of f; that is, it may exclude certain numbers that are in the domain of f, because the limit defining the derivative does not exist at these numbers. We say that a function f is differentiable at those elements in its domain where $f'(x)$ exists. Thus the domain of f' is that subset of the domain of f comprising the numbers at which f is differentiable.

Example 1

Example 1

The derived function f' of the function

$$f : x \longmapsto x \qquad (x \in R)$$

is given by:

$$f'(x) = \lim_{h \to 0} \frac{(x + h) - x}{h} = \lim_{h \to 0} \frac{h}{h} = 1$$

and the limit exists for all $x \in R$: so the domain of f' is also R.

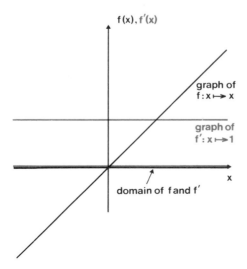

Example 2

Example 2

The derived function g' of the modulus function

$$g : x \longmapsto |x| \qquad (x \in R)$$

is given (where it exists) by:

$$g'(x) = \lim_{h \to 0} \frac{|x + h| - |x|}{h}.$$

The evaluation of this limit, though not difficult, is a little tedious (see text following this example). A simpler method of finding the domain of g' is to use the graph of g. The graph below shows the point $(0, 0)$ at which there is no tangent; since the slope of the tangent coincides with the value of the derivative, we see that there is no derivative, i.e. the limit does not exist near $x = 0$. At all other points there is a tangent (in fact it coincides with part of the graph) and so the function is differentiable everywhere except at $x = 0$. Thus the domain of g' consists of the set R with 0 omitted.

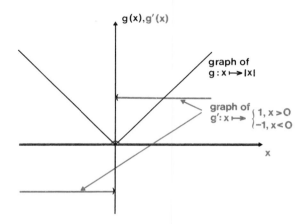

Like all arguments based on graphs (or figures in general), the one given in Example 2 makes use of geometrical intuition and it is therefore a demonstration (in the sense defined in section 7.2.3 of *Unit 7, Sequences and Limits I*) rather than a proof. For a proof we must go back to the definition and evaluate the limit. We consider three cases:

Discussion
* *

(i) $x > 0$

In evaluating the limit it is only small values of $|h|$ that matter; so we need only consider $h > -x$, so that $h + x > 0$. It follows that $|x| = x$ and $|x + h| = x + h$; the definition of $f'(x)$ therefore gives

$$f'(x) = \lim_{h \to 0} \frac{(x + h) - x}{h} = \frac{h}{h} = 1.$$

(ii) $x < 0$

Again, we need only consider small values of $|h|$. We take $h < -x$, so that $h + x < 0$. It follows that $|x| = -x$ and $|x + h| = -(x + h)$; so the expression for $f'(x)$ is

$$f'(x) = \lim_{h \to 0} \frac{|x + h| - |x|}{h} = \lim_{h \to 0} \frac{-(x + h) + x}{h} = \frac{-h}{h} = -1.$$

(iii) $x = 0$

The expression for $f'(x)$ is

$$f'(x) = \lim_{h \to 0} \frac{|h|}{h},$$

but since $\dfrac{|h|}{h}$ takes the value $+1$ for small positive h and -1 for small negative h, there is no number close to $\dfrac{|h|}{h}$ for *all* small h: that is, *the function* $x \longmapsto |x|$ *is not differentiable at* 0.

12.2.2 Differentiation of Polynomials

12.2.2

Discussion

You have already seen how to differentiate a few functions. The results are shown in the table: in each case f has domain R.

f	f'		Page Number
$x \longmapsto$ constant	$x \longmapsto 0$	$(x \in R)$	15
$x \longmapsto x$	$x \longmapsto 1$	$(x \in R)$	17
$x \longmapsto x^2$	$x \longmapsto 2x$	$(x \in R)$	16
$x \longmapsto x^3$	$x \longmapsto 3x^2$	$(x \in R)$	14
$x \longmapsto |x|$	$\begin{cases} x \longmapsto 1 & (x \in R^+) \\ x \longmapsto -1 & (x \in R^-) \end{cases}$		18

To work out each new derivative, when it is required, from the definition

$$f'(x) = \lim_{h \to 0} \frac{f(x+h) - f(x)}{h} = \lim_{h \to 0} \frac{\Delta_h f(x)}{h}$$

would be very laborious. It is much easier to work out in advance a system of rules which makes it possible to differentiate many functions from a knowledge of relatively few basic derivatives. To formulate these rules, we begin with a class of particularly simple functions, namely the *polynomial functions*. The definition of a real polynomial function was given in *Unit 4, Finite Differences*: it is any function of the form:

$$p : x \longmapsto a_n x^n + a_{n-1} x^{n-1} + \cdots + a_1 x + a_0 \qquad (x \in R)$$

where $a_0, a_1, \ldots, a_n \in R$.

We saw in *Unit 4* that the difference operator Δ_h applied to a polynomial function of degree $n (n \in Z^+)$ gives another polynomial function of degree $n - 1$. In view of the presence of Δ_h in the definition of $f'(x)$, it is not surprising that just the same thing happens when the polynomial is differentiated instead of differenced.

Exercise 1

Differentiate the function:

$$f : x \longmapsto ax^2 + bx + c \qquad (x \in R).$$ ■

Exercise 1
(3 minutes)

Rather than try to differentiate the general polynomial function of degree n immediately, let us begin with the simplest such polynomial function which is

$$x \longmapsto x^n \qquad (x \in R)$$

where n is any positive integer or zero. The cases $n = 0, 1, 2, 3$, have already been treated in various exercises and examples; so if you know the binomial theorem you should not find the general case difficult.

Main Text
* * *

(See RB9) *(continued on page 20)*

Solution 1 **Solution 1**

We must differentiate the function

$$f : x \longmapsto ax^2 + bx + c \quad (x \in R).$$

That is, we must find

$$f'(x) = \lim_{h \to 0} \frac{f(x + h) - f(x)}{h}$$

$$= \lim_{h \to 0} \frac{a(x + h)^2 + b(x + h) + c - (ax^2 + bx + c)}{h}$$

$$= \lim_{h \to 0} \frac{2axh + ah^2 + bh}{h}$$

$$= \lim_{h \to 0} (2ax + ah + b)$$

$$= 2ax + b.$$

The derived function is, therefore:

$$f' : x \longmapsto 2ax + b \quad (x \in R).$$

Notice that if we write

$$f_1 : x \longmapsto ax^2, f_2 : x \longmapsto bx, f_3 : x \longmapsto c \quad (x \in R),$$

then

$$f = f_1 + f_2 + f_3$$

and

$$f' = f'_1 + f'_2 + f'_3. \qquad \blacksquare$$

(*continued from page 19*)

Exercise 2

Exercise 2
(2 minutes)

Differentiate the function:

$$f : x \longmapsto x^n \quad (x \in R)$$

where n is any positive integer or zero. $\qquad \blacksquare$

Extending the f' notation for derived functions, we can write the result of Exercise 2:

Main Text
* * *

$$(x \longmapsto x^n)' = (x \longmapsto nx^{n-1}) \quad (x \in R).$$

* * *

Some of the results obtained earlier (for example, the derivative of a constant function is zero, the derivative of $t \longmapsto t^3$ is $t \longmapsto 3t^2$) are special cases of this important result. The general polynomial

$$p(x) = a_n x^n + a_{n-1} x^{n-1} + \cdots + a_1 x + a_0$$

can be built up from "elementary" polynomials of the form x^k by first multiplying each of these elementary polynomials by the appropriate coefficient a_k to get one of the terms $a_k x^k$ in the general polynomial, and then adding all these terms together. By the corresponding operations on the "elementary" polynomial functions $x \longmapsto x^k$ we can build up the general polynomial function:

$$p : x \longmapsto a_n x^n + a_{n-1} x^{n-1} + \cdots + a_1 x + a_0 \quad (x \in R).$$

It follows that we shall also be able to build up the derived function p' provided we can obtain rules enabling us to deduce:

(i) the derived function of $x \longmapsto a_k x^k$ from that of $x \longmapsto x^k$,

(ii) the derived function of a sum of functions from the derived functions of its individual terms.

(Notice that this procedure is exactly the same as that adopted when differencing polynomials in *Unit 4, Finite Differences*, when calculating limits in *Unit 7, Sequences and Limits I*, when calculating definite integrals in *Unit 9, Integration I* and when discussing switching circuits and other systems in *Unit 11, Logic I*. In each case we deal with "complicated" expressions by breaking them up into "simpler" ones, dealing with these and then finding rules, usually in the form of morphisms, for putting the results together to obtain the result for the "complicated" expression.) Perhaps you would like to guess these rules for yourself.

Exercise 3

Guess the correct expressions to put in the boxes:

(i) For any non-zero number a and any function f, the derived function of $t \longmapsto af(t)$ is ☐ where $t \in$ (domain of f').

(ii) For any two functions f and g with the same domain, the derived function of $t \longmapsto f(t) + g(t)$ is ☐ where $t \in$ (intersection of the domains of f' and g'). Is the function $t \longmapsto f(t) + g(t)$ necessarily differentiable in this domain? ∎

Exercise 3
(3 minutes)

Exercise 4

Using the definition of a derivative, prove or disprove the guesses you made in the preceding exercise. ∎

Exercise 4
(5 minutes)

Exercise 5

Express the derivative of $f + g$ in terms of f' and g'. ∎

Exercise 5
(1 minute)

We can state the two rules of differentiation given in Exercise 3 as follows:

Main Text
* * *

First Rule of Differentiation

$(af)' = af'$, i.e. multiplying any function by a number multiplies its derived function by the same number.

Rule 1
* * *

Second Rule of Differentiation

$(f + g)' = f' + g'$, i.e. the derived function of a sum of functions is the sum of the individual derived functions, provided the domains are appropriate.

Rule 2
* * *

The second rule can be extended to cover any (finite) number of terms in a sum. We can now construct a derivative for the general polynomial

$$p : x \longmapsto a_n x^n + a_{n-1} x^{n-1} + \cdots + a_1 x + a_0 \quad (x \in R).$$

We have already shown that

$$(x \longmapsto x^k)' = x \longmapsto k x^{k-1} \quad (x \in R).$$

By Rule 1, multiplying a function by a constant (in this case a_k), multiplies its derived function by the same constant, so

$$(x \longmapsto a_k x^k)' = x \longmapsto k a_k x^{k-1} \quad (x \in R).$$

By Rule 2, the derived function of a sum of two or more functions is the sum of their individual derived functions. The polynomial function p is the sum of the functions $(x \longmapsto a_n x^n)$, $(x \longmapsto a_{n-1} x^{n-1})$ etc.; therefore its derivative is the sum of their derivatives:

$$p' = (x \longmapsto n a_n x^{n-1}) + (x \longmapsto (n-1) a_{n-1} x^{n-2}) + \cdots$$
$$+ (x \longmapsto a_1)$$

that is,

$$p' = x \longmapsto (n a_n x^{n-1} + (n-1) a_{n-1} x^{n-2} + \cdots + 2 a_2 x + a_1)$$
$$(x \in R).$$

Solution 2 Solution 2

$$f'(x) = \lim_{h \to 0} \frac{(x + h)^n - x^n}{h}$$

$$= \lim_{h \to 0} \frac{\left\{ x^n + nx^{n-1}h + \frac{n(n-1)}{2}x^{n-2}h^2 + \cdots + h^n \right\} - x^n}{h}$$

(by the binomial theorem)

$$= \lim_{h \to 0} \left\{ nx^{n-1} + \frac{n(n-1)}{2}x^{n-2}h + \cdots + h^{n-1} \right\}$$

(on dividing by h, since $h \neq 0$)

$$= nx^{n-1}$$

(by the methods of *Unit 7, Sequences and Limits I*).

Consequently the derived function of

$$x \longmapsto x^n \quad (x \in R)$$

is

$$x \longmapsto nx^{n-1} \quad (x \in R)$$

Solution 3 Solution 3

(i) $t \longmapsto af'(t)$
(ii) $t \longmapsto f'(t) + g'(t)$.

The function $t \longmapsto f(t) + g(t)$ is always differentiable, where $t \in$ (intersection of domains of f' and g').

Solution 4 Solution 4

We use the rules for addition and multiplication of limits of functions, which are similar to those for limits of sequences given in *Unit 7, Sequences and Limits I*.

(i) When $t \in$ (domain of f') then

$$\lim_{h \to 0} \left(\frac{af(t + h) - af(t)}{h} \right) = \lim_{h \to 0} \left(a \left[\frac{f(t + h) - f(t)}{h} \right] \right)$$

$$= \lim_{h \to 0} (a) \times \lim_{h \to 0} \left(\frac{f(t + h) - f(t)}{h} \right)$$

$$= af'(t).$$

(ii) When $t \in$ (intersection of domains of f' and g'), then

$$\lim_{h \to 0} \left(\frac{\{ f(t + h) + g(t + h) \} - \{ (f(t) + g(t)) \}}{h} \right)$$

$$= \lim_{h \to 0} \left(\frac{f(t + h) - f(t)}{h} + \frac{g(t + h) - g(t)}{h} \right)$$

$$= \lim_{h \to 0} \left(\frac{f(t + h) - f(t)}{h} \right) + \lim_{h \to 0} \left(\frac{g(t + h) - g(t)}{h} \right)$$

$$= f'(t) + g'(t).$$

Solution 5 Solution 5

This is just a formal statement of the result of Exercise 3 part (ii).

$$(f + g)'(t) = f'(t) + g'(t)$$

($t \in$ intersection of domains of f' and g').

Exercise 6

(i) Differentiate

$$x \longmapsto 10x^5 + \tfrac{1}{8}x^3 + x \quad (x \in R).$$

(ii) Differentiate $x \longmapsto 2x + |x| \quad (x \in R)$ using the derived function calculated in Example 12.2.1.2. (Do not forget to determine the domain of the derived function, i.e. the subset of R for which the given function is differentiable.) ∎

12.2.3 The Differentiation Operator

We have seen in Section 12.2.1 that to every function f there corresponds a unique derived function, f', whose domain is a subset of the domain of f. (In some cases, this subset contains no elements, that is to say f cannot be differentiated anywhere. Can you think of an example? In case you cannot, you will find one in Example 1 below.)

That is, we have a rule which assigns to each member, f, of the set of real functions a unique function f'; the rule can be described by the word differentiate, and you may find it helpful to think of it as a machine which takes one function and turns it into another, as illustrated below:

INPUT   MACHINE   OUTPUT

Example 1

Example 1

An example of a function which cannot be differentiated anywhere in its domain is a function whose domain consists of isolated numbers, for example:

$$f:x \longmapsto x \quad (x \in \{1, 2, 3, 4\}).$$

The reason why this function cannot be differentiated is that the definition of a derivative at x involves taking the limit of

$$\frac{f(x + h) - f(x)}{h}$$

as h tends to zero. But this means that there must be some interval $[x - h, x + h]$ contained in the domain of f; otherwise we cannot apply our definition of a limit. But if x is one of the numbers 1, 2, 3 or 4, and $0 < |h| < 1$, then $x + h$ cannot be one of these numbers, so $f(x + h)$ is not defined; and hence the derivative at x does not exist. ∎

Here we have a situation very similar to one in *Unit 4, Finite Differences*, where we also had a rule for turning one function into another. There we defined the difference operator:

$$\Delta_h : f \longmapsto [x \longmapsto f(x + h) - f(x)] \quad (f \in F)$$

where F is the set of all real functions.

Here we shall do a similar thing: we define an operator D whose effect on any function in its domain is to differentiate it:

$$D : f \longmapsto f'.$$

It is called the differentiation operator. To complete the definition of the operator D we must specify its domain. We shall take this domain, as for Δ_h, to be the set of all real functions, F. Using the operator D we can write

(*continued on page 24*)

23

Solution 12.2.2.6 **Solution 12.2.2.6**

(i) Using the formula for the derivative of a polynomial function, the derived function of

$$x \longmapsto 10x^5 + \tfrac{1}{8}x^3 + x \quad (x \in R)$$

is

$$x \longmapsto 50x^4 + \tfrac{3}{8}x^2 + 1 \quad (x \in R).$$

(ii) Let $f : x \longmapsto 2x$, and $g : x \longmapsto |x|$ $(x \in R)$. Then $f' : x \longmapsto 2$ $(x \in R)$ and

$$\left. \begin{array}{ll} g' : x \longmapsto 1 & (x > 0) \\ x \longmapsto -1 & (x < 0) \end{array} \right\} \quad x \in R \wedge x \neq 0.^*$$

The intersection of the domains of f' and g' is equal to the domain of g'. So the derived function of $x \longmapsto 2x + |x|$ $(x \in R)$ is

$$x \longmapsto f'(x) + g'(x) \quad (x \in R \wedge x \neq 0),$$

i.e.

$$x \longmapsto \left\{ \begin{array}{ll} 3 & (x > 0) \\ 1 & (x < 0) \end{array} \right\} \quad (x \in R \wedge x \neq 0). \qquad \blacksquare$$

(continued from page 23)

the results of section 12.2.2 as follows:

$$D(x \longmapsto x^m) = x \longmapsto mx^{m-1}$$

$$D(af) = aDf \quad (a \in R \wedge f \in F)$$

$$D(f + g) = Df + Dg \quad (f \in F \wedge g \in F).$$

We have followed the same convention as in *Unit 4, Finite Differences*, writing Df as an abbreviation for $D(f)$; and we have written af as an abbreviation for the function $x \longmapsto af(x)$ $(x \in R)$. We also often drop the specification of the domain of the function being differentiated, as we have done in the first result above.

Exercise 1

Exercise 1
(2 minutes)

Using notation similar to that for the finite difference operator Δ_h, it is usual to write D^2 for $D \circ D$, D^3 for $D \circ D \circ D$, and so on.

(i) Evaluate $D^2 (x \longmapsto ax^2 + bx + c)$

(ii) Evaluate $D^3 (x \longmapsto x^3)$. $\qquad \blacksquare$

If f is any real function, the function D^2f is called the second derived function of f, D^3f is called the third derived function, and so on.

Main Text

Definition 2

In the notation used in section 12.2.1, we would write: f'' for D^2f; f''' or $f^{(3)}$ for D^3f; $f^{(4)}$ for D^4f; $f^{(n)}$ for D^nf, and so on.

Notation 1

One of the reasons for introducing the operator D is that it enables us to relate the properties of the differentiation mapping to those of other mappings we have met.

* The symbol $\wedge$ is defined in *Unit 11, Logic 1*; it means "and".

Exercise 2

Can you recognize the property of *D* expressed in the form:

$$D(f + g) = Df + Dg?$$ ■

Exercise 2
(3 minutes)

Discussion

There are other binary operations on the domain *F* of *D*, and it is natural to ask whether there are any more useful morphisms about. For instance, what about multiplication? Suppose we asked you to guess? Would you guess

$$D(f \times g) = Df \times Dg?$$

If you think that this guess is reasonable, then we suggest you work Exercise 3; incidentally, Leibniz, one of the inventors of calculus, thought it was reasonable at one time.

But we are really not tackling the problem correctly; the question we should ask first is: "Is *D* compatible with $\times$?" (For the definition of compatibility, see *Unit 3, Operations and Morphisms*.) If the answer is "No", then there is no morphism to be found. If the answer is "Yes", we can then go on to see if we recognize the induced binary operation. We ask you to investigate this in Exercise 4. The consequences of Exercises 3 and 4 are followed up in the next section.

Exercise 3

Show by an example (as simple as possible) that cases exist where

$$D(f \times g) \neq Df \times Dg$$

so that *D* is *not* a morphism of $(F, \times)$ to $(F_1, \times)$. ■

Exercise 3
(3 minutes)

Exercise 4

Is *D* compatible with multiplication? ■

Exercise 4
(5 minutes)

Hints for Exercises 3 and 4

(i) The definition of $f \times g$ is given in *Unit 1, Functions*.

(ii) Try $f_1 : x \longmapsto x \qquad (x \in R)$
and $g_1 : x \longmapsto 1 \qquad (x \in R)$ } in Exercise 3.

(iii) For Exercise 4 you may also find it helpful to try

$$f_2 : x \longmapsto x \quad (x \in R) \quad \text{and} \quad g_2 : x \longmapsto 2 \quad (x \in R).$$

Solution 1 **Solution 1**

(i) Let
$$f : x \longmapsto ax^2 + bx + c \quad (x \in R)$$
then
$$Df : x \longmapsto 2ax + b \quad (x \in R)$$
and
$$D^2 f : x \longmapsto 2a \quad (x \in R).$$

(ii)
$$f : x \longmapsto x^3 \quad (x \in R)$$
$$Df : x \longmapsto 3x^2 \quad (x \in R)$$
$$D^2 f : x \longmapsto 6x \quad (x \in R)$$
$$D^3 f : x \longmapsto 6 \quad (x \in R).$$

(Note the fact that we have included the somewhat trivial information $(x \in R)$ on every line, to emphasize that the domain stays the same throughout. It looks rather unnecessary here, but if we were differentiating more complicated functions we might well find that the domain changed in going from a function to its derived function.) ■

Solution 2 **Solution 2**

D is a *morphism* of $(F, +)$ to $(F_1, +)$, where F_1 is the set of images of elements of F, and $+$ denotes the addition of functions. D is many-one; for instance:
$$D(x \longmapsto x^2) = D(x \longmapsto x^2 + 2)$$
and so D is a homomorphism. ■

Solution 3 **Solution 3**

Using Hint (i), we try the functions:
$$f_1 : x \longmapsto x \quad (x \in R), \quad Df_1 : x \longmapsto 1 \quad (x \in R)$$
and
$$g_1 : x \longmapsto 1 \quad (x \in R), \quad Dg_1 : x \longmapsto 0 \quad (x \in R);$$
then
$$f_1 \times g_1 : x \longmapsto x \quad (x \in R), \quad D(f_1 \times g_1) : x \longmapsto 1 \quad (x \in R).$$
But
$$Df_1 \times Dg_1 = x \longmapsto 0 \quad (x \in R)$$
$$\neq D(f_1 \times g_1).$$
■

Solution 4 **Solution 4**

Recalling the definition of compatibility in *Unit 3, Operations and Morphisms*, we know that D is compatible with multiplication if, whenever
$$D(f_1) = D(f_2) \quad \text{and} \quad D(g_1) = D(g_2),$$
then
$$D(f_1 \times g_1) = D(f_2 \times g_2).$$

Now we cannot prove a formula true for all elements in a set simply by looking at some of the elements in the set, whereas we *can* prove it false by showing that it is false for some elements of the set. So the fact that Hint (iii) gives us particular examples should tell us that D is going to turn out *not* to be compatible with multiplication.

We could use the functions in Hints (ii) and (iii) as follows:

$$D(f_1) = D(f_2) = (x \longmapsto 1) \quad (x \in R)$$

$$D(g_1) = D(g_2) = (x \longmapsto 0) \quad (x \in R)$$

$$D(f_1 \times g_1) = (x \longmapsto 1) \quad (x \in R)$$

$$D(f_2 \times g_2) = (x \longmapsto 2) \quad (x \in R)$$

so

$$D(f_1 \times g_1) \neq D(f_2 \times g_2),$$

and so D is not compatible with multiplication.

An example such as this, which is used to show that a statement is false, is called a *counter-example*. ∎

12.2.4 Differentiation of Products

The result of the previous exercise has shown that differentiating the product of two functions is not going to be such an easy matter as differentiating their sum. In this section we shall investigate how to differentiate such a product.

We have already seen (in section 12.2.2) the usefulness of having a rule for differentiating a product of two polynomial functions when one of them is a constant function. The rule is

$$D(af) = aDf.$$

As long as we want to differentiate polynomial functions only, this is all we need to know about the derived function of a product, but to differentiate a function such as

$$x \longmapsto x \sin x \quad (x \in R)$$

which is a product of the two functions

$$x \longmapsto x \quad (x \in R)$$

and

$$x \longmapsto \sin x \quad (x \in R)$$

neither of which is a constant, we need a more general rule for differentiating products of functions.

Let us denote the two functions whose product we wish to differentiate by f and g, and their product by k, so that

$$f \times g = k.$$

We assume for simplicity that the functions have domain R. To illustrate the product relationship and the subsequent argument, we suppose that the elements of the domain of f, g and k are times (represented by a variable t), and that the images of t under the functions f, g and k are the sides and area of a rectangle:

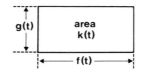

Our problem is to evaluate $k'(t)$, the rate at which the area changes with time. By the definition of a derivative, this is

$$k'(t) = \lim_{h \to 0} \frac{k(t + h) - k(t)}{h}$$

that is

$$k'(t) = \lim_{h \to 0} \frac{f(t + h)g(t + h) - f(t)g(t)}{h}.$$

Equation (1)

The numerator is the difference in area of two rectangles:

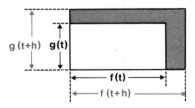

and is therefore equal to the area of the shaded L-shaped strip in the above diagram. This strip can be treated as the sum of three rectangles, as shown below:

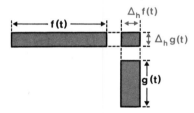

(Remember that $\Delta_h f(t) = f(t + h) - f(t)$.)

Adding the areas of the rectangles and substituting in Equation (1), we get

$$k'(t) = \lim_{h \to 0} \frac{f(t)\Delta_h g(t) + g(t)\Delta_h f(t) + \Delta_h g(t)\Delta_h f(t)}{h}$$

Equation (2)

$$= f(t) \lim_{h \to 0} \frac{\Delta_h g(t)}{h} + g(t) \lim_{h \to 0} \frac{\Delta_h f(t)}{h} + \lim_{h \to 0} \frac{\Delta_h g(t)\Delta_h f(t)}{h},$$

by the rules for limits given in *Unit 7, Sequences and Limits I* (since $f(t)$ and $g(t)$ do not involve h). Hence

$$k'(t) = f(t)g'(t) + g(t)f'(t) + \lim_{h \to 0} \frac{\Delta_h g(t)\Delta_h f(t)}{h},$$

Equation (3)

by the definition of a derivative.

The last term on the right-hand side can be written

$$\lim_{h \to 0} \frac{\Delta_h f(t)}{h} \times \lim_{h \to 0} \Delta_h g(t) = f'(t) \times 0 = 0,$$

since both these limits exist and

$$\lim_{h \to 0} \Delta_h g(t) = \lim_{h \to 0} [g(t + h) - g(t)] = 0,$$

if g is a continuous function.* (In fact, this is not a new assumption since we have already assumed that g is differentiable, and it can be proved without much difficulty that every differentiable function is continuous: a result which is intuitively obvious if we regard differentiability in terms of being able to draw tangents.)

Equation (3), therefore, becomes

$$k'(t) = f(t)g'(t) + g(t)f'(t).$$

Equation (4)

That is, the rate of change of the area of the rectangle is the sum of two terms: the rate at which area is being added because the length of the side of original length $f(t)$ is increasing, plus the rate at which area is being added because the length of the side of original length $g(t)$ is increasing.

Equation (4) is the rule for differentiating products. We have thought of t as a time in deriving this rule, but the rectangle illustration can be dropped† and the mathematical argument applies to any product of functions with domain R or some subset of R. The Product Rule can, of course, also be written in terms of the functions themselves instead of images; it then takes the form:

$$(fg)' = fg' + gf'$$

Product Rule
* * *

or, in terms of D:

$$D(fg) = f\,Dg + g\,Df.$$

This can be regarded as a generalization of the equation $D(af) = a\,Df$, to which it reduces when g is a constant function.

Exercise 1

What can you say about the domain of $(fg)'$ in terms of the domain of f' and g'? ■

Exercise 1
(5 minutes)

Exercise 2

Verify the product rule by considering the product of the two functions:

$$f: x \longmapsto 2x + 1 \qquad (x \in R)$$

$$g: x \longmapsto x - 1 \qquad (x \in R). \qquad ■$$

Exercise 2
(2 minutes)

---

* Notice that we have to assume that g is continuous in order to be sure that $\lim\limits_{h \to 0} g(t + h) = g(t)$.

If g is not continuous, then this limit may exist and be different from $g(t)$: see examples in *Unit 7, Sequences and Limits I*.

† Note that we could write Equation (1) in the form:

$$k'(t) = \lim_{h \to 0} \frac{f(t + h)g(t + h) - f(t)g(t + h) + f(t)g(t + h) - f(t)g(t)}{h},$$

i.e.

$$k'(t) = \lim_{h \to 0} \frac{\Delta_h f(t)g(t + h) + f(t)\Delta_h g(t)}{h}$$

which again leads us to Equation (4).

Solution 1 **Solution 1**

The domain of the function $(fg)' = fg' + gf'$ is the intersection of the domains of f, f', g and g'. But since the domain of f' is contained in the domain of f, and the domain of g' is contained in that of g, we can simplify this: the required domain is the intersection of the domains of f' and g'.

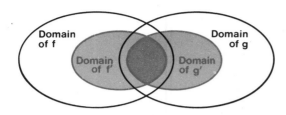

Solution 2 **Solution 2**

$$fg : x \longmapsto 2x^2 - x - 1 \qquad (x \in R)$$

$$(fg)' : x \longmapsto 4x - 1 \qquad (x \in R)$$

$$f(x)g'(x) + g(x)f'(x) = (2x + 1)g'(x) + (x - 1)f'(x)$$

$$= (2x + 1)1 + (x - 1)2$$

$$= 4x - 1.$$

Thus

$$(fg' + gf') : x \longmapsto 4x - 1 \qquad (x \in R),$$

and the result is verified.

12.2.5   Differentiation of Composite Functions

In the last two sections we have shown that D is a morphism with respect to addition of functions in its domain and codomain, but that no morphism exists for multiplication. We shall deal with division later, and subtraction follows directly from addition to give

$$D(f - g) = D(f + (-g)) \quad \text{where} \; -g : x \longmapsto -g(x)$$

$$= Df + D(-g)$$

$$= Df - Dg$$

using the rule $D(ag) = aDg$, with $a = -1$.

The last of the binary operations on functions that we defined in *Unit 1, Functions* was the operation of composition

$$f \circ g : x \longmapsto f(g(x)).$$

We approach the investigation of composition in the same way as we tackled that of multiplication.

Exercise 1

Show by as simple an example as possible, that cases exist where

$$D(f \circ g) \neq Df \circ Dg,$$

so that D is not a morphism with respect to composition of the functions in its domain and codomain.

Exercise 2

Exercise 2
(5 minutes)

Is *D* compatible with composition? ■

So we must try to find a rule for differentiating the composite of two functions *f* and *g*. We write

Main Text
* * *

$$f \circ g = k, \quad \text{i.e.} f \circ g(x) = f(g(x)) = k(x).$$

The relation between these functions is illustrated below:

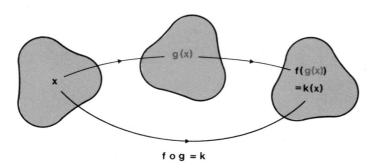

$$f \circ g = k$$

It can also be illustrated in this way:

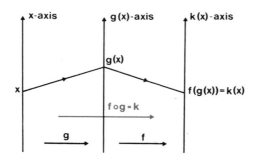

To determine whether $f \circ g$ is differentiable we consider the formula defining a derivative:

$$k'(x) = \lim_{h \to 0} \frac{k(x + h) - k(x)}{h}.$$

The limit on the right can be interpreted using a diagram similar to the one below:

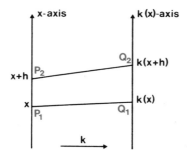

We see that

$$\frac{k(x + h) - k(x)}{h} = \frac{Q_1 Q_2}{P_1 P_2}.$$

This may remind you of the scale factor of *k* at *x*, which we defined in *Unit 2, Errors and Accuracy*. Here we shall refer to it as the magnification produced by the function *k* when it maps the segment $P_1 P_2$ (i.e. the interval $[x, x + h]$) to the segment $Q_1 Q_2$ (i.e. the interval $[k(x), k(x + h)]$).

Definition 1

(*continued on page 32*)

31

Solution 1

Almost any example will do; here is one:

Let

$$g : x \longmapsto 1 \quad (x \in R), \qquad g' : x \longmapsto 0 \quad (x \in R);$$

$$f : x \longmapsto x \quad (x \in R), \qquad f' : x \longmapsto 1 \quad (x \in R);$$

$$f \circ g : x \longmapsto 1 \quad (x \in R);$$

$$(f \circ g)' : x \longmapsto 0 \quad (x \in R), \qquad f' \circ g' : x \longmapsto 1 \quad (x \in R).$$

So $D(f \circ g) \neq Df \circ Dg$ in this case.

Solution 2

According to the definition of compatibility given in *Unit 3, Operations and Morphisms*, D is compatible with composition if, whenever

$$Df_1 = Df_2 \quad \text{and} \quad Dg_1 = Dg_2$$

then

$$D(f_1 \circ g_1) = D(f_2 \circ g_2).$$

It can be shown by counter-examples that this condition is not satisfied; for example:

$$f_1 : x \longmapsto x^2 + 1 \quad (x \in R), \qquad g_1 : x \longmapsto x \quad (x \in R);$$

$$f_2 : x \longmapsto x^2 \quad (x \in R), \qquad g_2 : x \longmapsto x + 1 \quad (x \in R);$$

$$f_1 \circ g_1 : x \longmapsto x^2 + 1 \quad (x \in R),$$

$$f_2 \circ g_2 : x \longmapsto (x + 1)^2 \quad (x \in R);$$

$$D(f_1 \circ g_1) : x \longmapsto 2x \quad (x \in R),$$

$$D(f_2 \circ g_2) : x \longmapsto 2x + 2 \quad (x \in R).$$

■

(*continued from page 31*)

Our problem is to express the derived function of $f \circ g$ in terms of the functions f and g: in terms of diagrams, it is to combine the last two diagrams. We can combine the two diagrams in the following way:

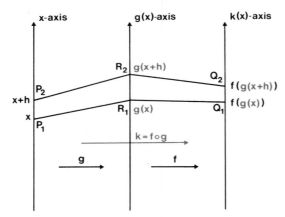

Instead of performing the mapping k in one stage we perform it in two stages: we perform first g and then f. Thus the segment $P_1 P_2$ is mapped first to the segment $R_1 R_2$ and then to the segment $Q_1 Q_2$. The magnifications produced in these two steps are

$$\frac{R_1 R_2}{P_1 P_2} \quad \text{and} \quad \frac{Q_1 Q_2}{R_1 R_2}$$

respectively, and the overall magnification is the product of these two:

$$\frac{Q_1 Q_2}{P_1 P_2} = \frac{R_1 R_2}{P_1 P_2} \times \frac{Q_1 Q_2}{R_1 R_2}.$$

Equation (1)

We have

$$\lim_{h \to 0} \frac{Q_1 Q_2}{P_1 P_2} = k'(x).$$

For the magnification in the first stage of the two-stage process we have

$$\lim_{h \to 0} \frac{R_1 R_2}{P_1 P_2} = g'(x).$$

Finally, the magnification produced by the function f has the limit

$$\lim_{h \to 0} \frac{Q_1 Q_2}{R_1 R_2} = f'(g(x))^*.$$

This time the derivative has to be computed at $g(x)$ and not at x, since the point R_1 corresponds to the number $g(x)$.

If we put these three limits together we obtain from Equation (1) the Composite Function Rule:

$$k'(x) = g'(x) \times f'(g(x)).$$

Composite Function Rule
* * *

In function notation, we have:

$$(f \circ g)' = (f' \circ g) \times g'.$$

* * *

It is often called the chain rule, or "function of a function" rule, since a composite function is, in a sense, a function of a function.

Example 1

Example 1

Differentiate

$$k : x \longmapsto (2x + 1)^2 \quad (x \in R).$$

(This could be done by expanding the brackets, but we shall apply the above rule.)

If we let

$$g : x \longmapsto 2x + 1 \quad (x \in R)$$

and

$$f : x \longmapsto x^2 \qquad (x \in R)$$

then $k = f \circ g$.

We can now use the composite function rule, i.e.

$$k' = (f' \circ g) \times g'$$
$$= [(x \longmapsto 2x) \circ (x \longmapsto 2x + 1)] \times (x \longmapsto 2)$$
$$= x \longmapsto 2(2x + 1) \times 2$$
$$= x \longmapsto 4(2x + 1) \qquad (x \in R). \qquad \blacksquare$$

Exercise 3

Exercise 3
(3 minutes)

If

$$f : x \longmapsto x^2 + 1 \quad (x \in R)$$

and

$$g : x \longmapsto x^2 - 1 \quad (x \in R),$$

find $f \circ g$.

Differentiate $f \circ g$ directly and also using the composite function rule. Compare the two results. $\qquad \blacksquare$

---

* This step really covers up the difficult part of the verification, which depends on the continuity of g. A formal proof can be found in *Calculus* by T. M. Apostol (see Bibliography).

Solution 3

The steps in the calculation can be represented diagrammatically as shown:

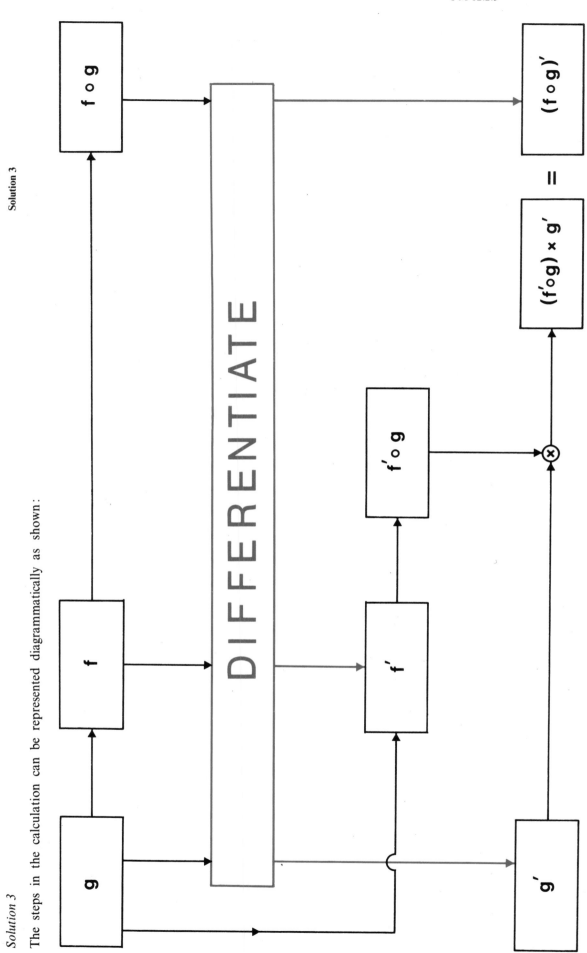

Solution 3

For the specific functions in this exercise (the domain is R in each case) this becomes:

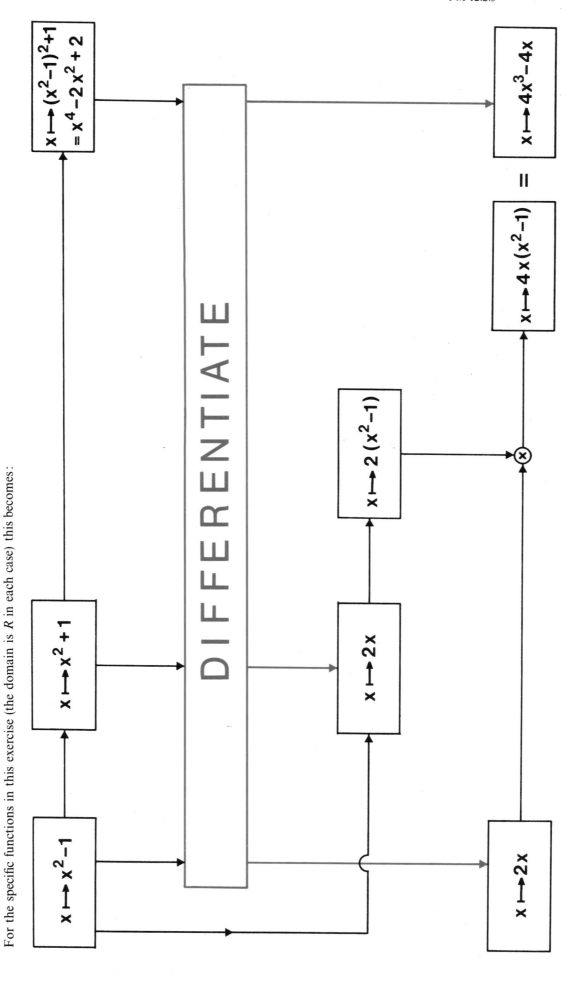

Exercise 4*

Differentiate:

(i) $k_1 : x \longmapsto (x+1)^5 \qquad (x \in R)$

(ii) $k_2 : x \longmapsto (3x+1)^5 \qquad (x \in R).$ ∎

Exercise 4
(3 minutes)

Exercise 5

Differentiate:

(i) $k_1 : x \longmapsto (7x+3)^5 \qquad (x \in R)$

(ii) $k_2 : x \longmapsto (2x^2+3x+2)^2 \qquad (x \in R).$ ∎

Exercise 5
(3 minutes)

12.2.6 Differentiation of Quotients

12.2.6

Main Text
* * *

In this section and the next we complete the list of rules of differentiation by deducing from the product rule a rule for differentiating the quotient of two functions, and deducing from the composite function rule a rule for differentiating inverse functions. You are not expected to be able to deduce these rules but you are expected to know the results and how to use them.

We begin by finding the derived function of the reciprocal function, which we denote here by the letter r, so that

$$r : x \longmapsto \frac{1}{x} \qquad (x \in R \wedge x \neq 0);$$

then

$$r'(x) = \lim_{h \to 0} \left(\frac{r(x+h) - r(x)}{h} \right)$$

$$= \lim_{h \to 0} \frac{1}{h} \left(\frac{1}{x+h} - \frac{1}{x} \right) \quad \text{(by definition of } r\text{)}$$

$$= \lim_{h \to 0} \frac{1}{h} \left(\frac{x - (x+h)}{(x+h)x} \right)$$

$$= \lim_{h \to 0} \left(\frac{-h}{h(x+h)x} \right)$$

$$= \lim_{h \to 0} \left(\frac{-1}{(x+h)x} \right) \quad \text{(the cancellation of the } h\text{'s is valid since } h \neq 0).$$

Taking the limit as $h \rightsquigarrow 0$ we obtain (since $x \neq 0$)

$$r'(x) = \frac{-1}{x^2}$$

i.e.

$$D\left(x \longmapsto \frac{1}{x} \right) = x \longmapsto \frac{-1}{x^2}$$

or

$$r' = -r \times r,$$

the domain being the set of non-zero real numbers throughout.

---

* You may like to use the diagrams at the back of this text.

Note

(i) We shall denote the product function $r \times r$ by r^2.
Thus
$$r^2 : x \longmapsto r(x) \times r(x) = (r(x))^2.$$

(ii) If
$$v : x \longmapsto v(x), \qquad (x \in R)$$

then we shall denote the function:
$$x \longmapsto \frac{1}{v(x)} \qquad (x \in R \wedge v(x) \neq 0)$$

by $\frac{1}{v}$.

We can now apply our last result to the differentiation of the quotient of two functions. If two functions u and v have as domain the same subset of R, and codomain R, then we define their quotient, $\frac{u}{v}$ or u/v, by

$$\frac{u}{v} : x \longmapsto \frac{u(x)}{v(x)} \quad (x \in \text{domain of } u \text{ and } v, \wedge v(x) \neq 0).$$

The formula for differentiating such functions is a useful one. It may help you to remember the rule if you work it out for yourself: so the rest of the derivation of this formula is set as an exercise.

Exercise 1

Denoting the reciprocal function by r as in the text, we can write

$$\frac{u}{v} = u \times \frac{1}{v} = u \times (r \circ v).$$

Using the following results:
 (i) the derived function of r is $-r^2$.
(ii) the product rule, i.e.
$$(f \times g)' = f' \times g + f \times g',$$

(iii) the composite function rule, i.e.
$$(f \circ g)' = (f' \circ g) \times g',$$

express $\left(\dfrac{u}{v}\right)$ in terms of u', v', u and v. ∎

The result of the last exercise gives the Quotient Rule:

$$\left(\frac{u}{v}\right)' = \frac{u' \times v - u \times v'}{v^2}$$

which means that

if $\qquad w(x) = \dfrac{u(x)}{v(x)}$

then

$$w'(x) = \frac{u'(x) \times v(x) - u(x) \times v'(x)}{(v(x))^2}.$$

The domain of $\left(\dfrac{u}{v}\right)'$ is the intersection of the domain of u', the domain of v', and the set $\{x : x \in R, v(x) \neq 0\}$.

(continued on page 40)

Solution 12.2.5.4

Solution 12.2.5.4

(i) Let

$$f_1 : x \longmapsto x^5 \qquad (x \in R)$$

$$g_1 : x \longmapsto x + 1 \quad (x \in R).$$

Adopting the schematic form of the previous exercise, we now have:
(*See illustration on opposite page*)

(ii) We can repeat the process with

$$f_2 : x \longmapsto x^5 \qquad (x \in R)$$

$$g_2 : x \longmapsto 3x + 1 \quad (x \in R).$$

Alternatively, we notice that

$$k_2(x) = k_1(3x)$$

so that we can write

$$k_2 = k_1 \circ (x \longmapsto 3x)$$

whence

$$\begin{aligned}
k_2' &= [k_1' \circ (x \longmapsto 3x)] \times (x \longmapsto 3) \\
&= [x \longmapsto 5(3x + 1)^4] \times (x \longmapsto 3) \\
&= x \longmapsto 15(3x + 1)^4 \quad (x \in R).
\end{aligned}$$

In general, if

$$k_2(x) = k_1(ax)$$

so that

$$k_2 = k_1 \circ (x \longmapsto ax)$$

we have

$$k_2' = [k_1' \circ (x \longmapsto ax)] \times (x \longmapsto a)$$

so that

$$k_2'(x) = ak_1'(ax). \qquad \blacksquare$$

Solution 12.2.5.5

Solution 12.2.5.5

(i) $x \longmapsto 35(7x + 3)^4 \qquad (x \in R)$

(ii) $x \longmapsto (8x + 6)(2x^2 + 3x + 2) \quad (x \in R).$ $\qquad \blacksquare$

Solution 1

Solution 1

$$\begin{aligned}
\left(\frac{u}{v}\right)' &= [u \times (r \circ v)]' = u' \times (r \circ v) + u \times (r \circ v)' \qquad \text{by (ii)} \\
&= u' \times (r \circ v) + u \times [(r' \circ v) \times v'] \qquad \text{by (iii)} \\
&= u' \times (r \circ v) + u \times (-r^2 \circ v) \times v'.
\end{aligned}$$

Now $r \circ v = \dfrac{1}{v}$ and $-r^2 \circ v = \dfrac{-1}{v^2}$, so that

$$\begin{aligned}
\left(\frac{u}{v}\right)' &= \frac{u'}{v} - \frac{u \times v'}{v^2} \\
&= \frac{u' \times v - v' \times u}{v^2}. \qquad \blacksquare
\end{aligned}$$

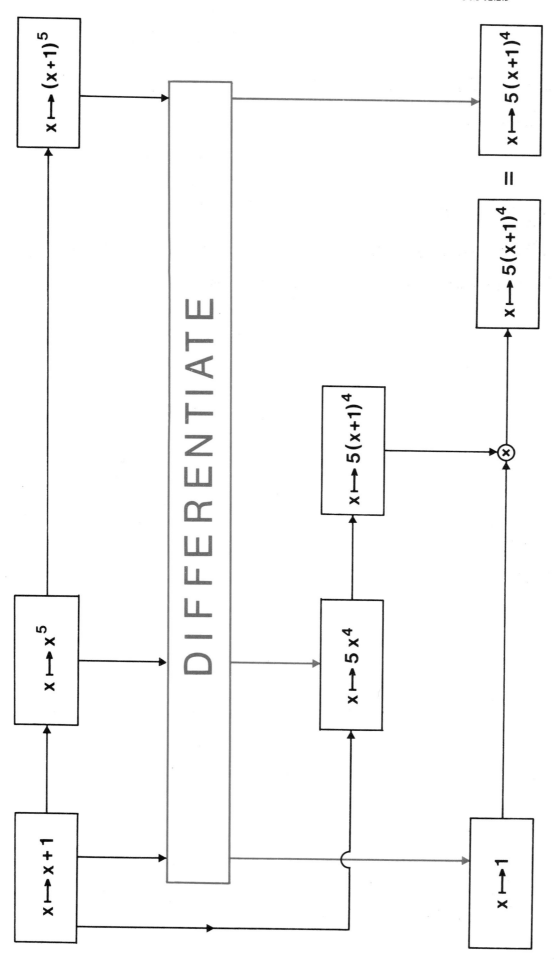

Exercise 2

Differentiate:

$$x \longmapsto \frac{1}{x^k} \qquad (x \in R \land x \neq 0)$$

where k is a positive integer.

Exercise 3

Differentiate:

(i) $w_1 : x \longmapsto \dfrac{-2}{2x+1} \qquad (x \in R \land x \neq -\frac{1}{2})$.

(ii) $w_2 : x \longmapsto \dfrac{2x-1}{2x+1} \qquad (x \in R \land x \neq -\frac{1}{2})$.

Can you see why the two results are the same?

Exercise 2

12.2.7 Differentiation of Inverse Functions

The last rule of differentiation we shall consider is the rule for differentiating the inverse of a function. The inverse of a one–one function, as defined in *Unit 1, Functions*, is a function that reverses the effect of the original one. For example, the inverse of the function "double the number" is the function "halve the number", since if we double a number and halve the result we come back to the original number. We saw in *Unit 1*, that a function has an inverse if and only if it is one–one; that is, if each element in the domain has a different image.

It follows that if g is the inverse of f, then

$$g \circ f : x \longmapsto x \qquad (x \in \text{domain of } f)$$

and

$$f \circ g : x \longmapsto x \qquad (x \in \text{domain of } g).$$

We can use the composite rule to find the derivative of g in terms of

$$f \circ g = x \longmapsto x$$

therefore

$$(f \circ g)' = x \longmapsto 1$$

and by the composite rule,

$$(f \circ g)' = (f' \circ g) \times g'$$

which gives us the Inverse Function Rule:

$$g' = \frac{x \longmapsto 1}{f' \circ g} = \frac{1}{f' \circ g}.$$

Notice that we have to take care with the domain of g': it is that part of the domain of g for which g is differentiable and for which $f' \circ g(x)$ does not vanish.*

Exercise 1

Differentiate

$$x \longmapsto x^{1/m} \qquad\qquad (x \in R^+)$$

where m is any positive integer. Compare your result with our previous result, namely

$$(x \longmapsto x^n)' = (x \longmapsto n x^{n-1}) \quad (x \in R \wedge x \neq 0)$$

where n is an integer. ■

* We also assume, here and everywhere else where we differentiate a composite function, that $f' \circ g$ is meaningful; i.e. that the domain of f' contains the image of the domain of g.

Solution 12.2.6.2
Solution 12.2.6.2

There are many ways of tackling this: we shall use the quotient rule with

$$u : x \longmapsto 1 \qquad (x \in R \wedge x \neq 0)$$

$$v : x \longmapsto x^k \qquad (x \in R \wedge x \neq 0).$$

We already know that

$$v' : x \longmapsto k x^{k-1} \qquad (x \in R \wedge x \neq 0)$$

so that

$$\frac{u'(x) \times v(x) - u(x) \times v'(x)}{v^2} = \frac{0 \times x^k - 1 \times k x^{k-1}}{x^{2k}}$$

$$= -k x^{-k-1}$$

$$= \frac{-k}{x^{k+1}}.$$

Considering the form $-k x^{-k-1}$, and remembering that we were differentiating $x \longmapsto x^{-k}$ ($x \in R \wedge x \neq 0$), we can see that we can now write

$$D(x \longmapsto x^n) = x \longmapsto n x^{n-1}$$

for any integral value of n,
(the domain is the set of non-zero real numbers when n is negative). ∎

Solution 12.2.6.3
Solution 12.2.6.3

The answer to both parts is

$$x \longmapsto \frac{4}{(2x + 1)^2} \qquad (x \in R \wedge x \neq -\tfrac{1}{2}).$$

The two results are the same because $w_1 - w_2$ is a constant function:

$$w_2(x) - w_1(x) = \frac{2x - 1}{2x + 1} + \frac{2}{2x + 1}$$

$$= \frac{(2x + 1) - 2}{2x + 1} + \frac{2}{2x + 1}$$

$$= 1$$

so that

$$w_2 - w_2 = x \longmapsto 1 \qquad (x \in R \wedge x \neq -\tfrac{1}{2})$$

whence

$$(w_2 - w_1)' = w_2' - w_1' = (x \longmapsto 1)' = x \longmapsto 0$$

i.e.

$$w_2'(x) - w_1'(x) = 0$$

or

$$w_2'(x) = w_1'(x). \qquad \blacksquare$$

Solution 1
Solution 1

Call the given function g. Then the inverse, f, of g is given by

$$f : x \longmapsto x^m \qquad (x \in R^+),$$

so that

$$f' : x \longmapsto m x^{m-1} \qquad (x \in R^+).$$

The inverse function rule then gives

$$g'(x) = \frac{1}{m(x^{1/m})^{m-1}}$$

$$= \frac{1}{m} \times \frac{1}{x^{(1-1/m)}}$$

$$= \frac{1}{m} x^{1/m-1}$$

i.e.

$$g' : x \longmapsto \frac{1}{m} x^{1/m-1}$$

We have shown that the result:

the derivative of $x \longmapsto x^n$ is $x \longmapsto nx^{n-1}$, where $n \in Z$, also holds when n is the reciprocal of a positive integer. ∎

12.3 STANDARD DERIVED FUNCTIONS

12.3

12.3.0 Introduction

12.3.0

Introduction
* *
Definition 1

The rules of differentiation obtained in the last section are sufficient for differentiating a rational function, that is, any function formed from polynomials by arithmetic operations (addition, multiplication, division) and by composition, and also for differentiating the inverse (if it exists) of such a function. This class of functions is quite extensive, but it does not include some very useful functions such as the trigonometric, exponential and logarithm functions. In the present section we shall fill some of the gaps. In each case it is the *result*, not the method of obtaining it, that you need to know, although we shall set some of the results as exercises so that you can get practice at applying the rules previously demonstrated. These standard derived functions are often called standard forms. In this section they are printed in red and for convenience they are also collected together, with a list of the rules of differentiation, at the end of this correspondence text, just before the appendices.

Definition 2
* * *

12.3.1 Trigonometric Functions

12.3.1

Main Text
* * *

Denoting the derived function of the sine function by sin', we have:

$$\sin' x = \lim_{h \to 0} \frac{\sin(x+h) - \sin x}{h}.$$

The evaluation of this limit involves some minor technicalities, which are not an essential part of the technique of differentiation and have therefore been excluded from this Foundation Course. (If you would like to read how the limit is evaluated, turn to Appendix II.) What does concern us here is the actual value of the limit: it turns out to be simply $\cos x$, so that the formula for differentiating sine is

$$\sin' x = \cos x \quad (x \in R)$$

or simply

$$\sin' = \cos.$$

We can also differentiate the function cos (i.e. $x \longmapsto \cos x \, (x \in R)$) using the limit definition of the derivative, but there is a possibly more elegant method which uses the identity:

$$\cos x = \sin\left(\frac{\pi}{2} - x\right) \quad (x \in R).$$

(See RB10)

Exercise 1

Exercise 1
(3 minutes)

Use the identity

$$\cos x = \sin\left(\frac{\pi}{2} - x\right) \quad (x \in R),$$

the composite function rule, and the fact that $\sin' = \cos$, to find the derivative of cos. ■

Exercise 2

Exercise 2
(3 minutes)

Differentiate the tan function. To do this you may need to use:

(i) $\tan x = \dfrac{\sin x}{\cos x}$,

(ii) the quotient rule,

(iii) the trigonometric identity $\cos^2 x + \sin^2 x = 1$.

(See RB10)

What is the domain of the tan function? What is the domain of its derived function? ■

Exercise 3

Exercise 3
(3 minutes)

Differentiate:

(i) $\sec = \dfrac{1}{\cos}$,

(ii) $\cot = \dfrac{1}{\tan}$,

(iii) $\operatorname{cosec} = \dfrac{1}{\sin}$.

The domain of the derived function is, in each case, the same as the domain of the original function. In cases (i) and (iii) the domain is R except for those numbers x for which $\cos x$ and $\sin x$ (respectively) are zero. In the case of (ii) the domain is R except for those numbers x for which $\tan x$ is undefined and for which $\tan x$ is zero. It is usual, however, to define $\cot x$ to be zero for those x for which $\tan x$ is undefined. ■

Exercise 4

Exercise 4
(3 minutes)

Find $D^2(\sin)$, $D^3(\sin)$, $D^4(\sin)$, $D^5(\sin)$. Generalize your results by writing down a formula for $D^n(\sin)$ that holds for every positive integer n. ■

Exercise 5 (Optional)

Exercise 5
(4 minutes)

Motions in which the position x of an object at time t is given by a formula such as

$$x - x_0 = a \sin b(t - t_0),$$

(where x_0, t_0, a and b are fixed numbers) are frequent in physics and mechanics. They are called simple harmonic motions. For example, any point on a clock pendulum or on a vibrating piano string executes a motion that is approximately simple harmonic. Calculate the velocity and also the acceleration (the rate of change of velocity) for a moving body whose position is given by the above formula, and find the function

Definition 1
*

Definition 2

$$(\text{position}) \longmapsto (\text{acceleration}).$$

The form of this function is characteristic of simple harmonic motion. ∎

Solution 1

Solution 1

Let

$$g : x \longmapsto \frac{\pi}{2} - x \quad (x \in R)$$

$$f : x \longmapsto \sin x \quad (x \in R).$$

Then using $(f \circ g)' = (f' \circ g) \times g'$, we have

$$\cos' = \left[\cos \circ \left(x \longmapsto \frac{\pi}{2} - x \right) \right] \times (x \longmapsto -1)$$

i.e.

$$\cos' x = -\cos \left(\frac{\pi}{2} - x \right).$$

This result can be simplified by noting that $\cos \left(\frac{\pi}{2} - x \right) = \sin x \ (x \in R)$, so that

$$\cos' = -\sin. \qquad \blacksquare$$

Solution 2

Solution 2

Starting with

$$\tan x = \frac{\sin x}{\cos x}$$

we have

$$\tan' x = \frac{\sin' x \cos x - \cos' x \sin x}{\cos^2 x} \quad \text{(quotient rule)}$$

$$= \frac{\cos^2 x + \sin^2 x}{\cos^2 x}$$

$$= \frac{1}{\cos^2 x} \qquad (\cos^2 x + \sin^2 x = 1)$$

$$= \sec^2 x \qquad \left(\sec x = \frac{1}{\cos x} \right).$$

This result can be written as

$$\tan' = \sec^2.$$

The domain of tan is R except for

$$\ldots, \frac{-5}{2}\pi, \frac{-3}{2}\pi, \frac{-1}{2}\pi, \frac{1}{2}\pi, \frac{3}{2}\pi, \frac{5}{2}\pi, \ldots.$$

The derived function has the same domain. $\qquad \blacksquare$

Solution 3

Solution 3

The rule for differentiating quotients of the form:

$$u(x) = \frac{v(x)}{w(x)} \quad (x \in R, \text{ where } w(x) \neq 0)$$

is

$$u'(x) = \frac{w(x)v'(x) - v(x)w'(x)}{(w(x))^2}$$

If $v(x) = 1$, $v'(x) = 0$, so that the quotient rule becomes:

$$u'(x) = \frac{-w'(x)}{(w(x))^2}$$

(i) When $u(x) = \dfrac{1}{\cos x}$, then $w(x) = \cos x$ and $w'(x) = -\sin x$, so that

$$u'(x) = \frac{\sin x}{\cos^2 x} = \sec x \tan x$$

i.e.

$$\sec' = \sec \tan$$

(ii) When $u(x) = \dfrac{1}{\tan x}$, then $w(x) = \tan x$ and $w'(x) = \sec^2 x$, so that

$$u'(x) = -\frac{\sec^2 x}{\tan^2 x} = -\frac{1}{\cos^2 x} \times \frac{\cos^2 x}{\sin^2 x} = \frac{-1}{\sin^2 x} = -\operatorname{cosec}^2 x$$

i.e.

$$\cot' = -\operatorname{cosec}^2$$

(iii) $u(x) = \dfrac{1}{\sin x}$; $w(x) = \sin x$; and so $w'(x) = \cos x$. Thus

$$u'(x) = -\frac{\cos x}{\sin^2 x} = -\operatorname{cosec} x \cot x$$

i.e.

$$\operatorname{cosec}' = -\operatorname{cosec} \cot. \qquad \blacksquare$$

Solution 4

Solution 4

$$D \sin = \cos$$
$$D^2 \sin = D \cos = -\sin$$
$$D^3 \sin = D(D^2 \sin) = D(-\sin) = -\cos$$
$$D^4 \sin = D(D^3 \sin) = D(-\cos) = \sin$$
$$D^5 \sin = D(D^4 \sin) = D(\sin) = \cos.$$

Suppose n is an *odd* integer i.e. we can write

$$n = 2k + 1 \quad \text{where } k \in \{0, 1, 2, \ldots\},$$

then

$$D^{2k+1} \sin = (-1)^k \cos.$$

If n is an *even* integer i.e. we can write

$$n = 2k, \quad (k \in \{1, 2, 3, \ldots\})$$

then

$$D^{2k} \sin = (-1)^k \sin. \qquad \blacksquare$$

Solution 5

Solution 5

The position of the object at time t is

$$x = x_0 + a \sin b(t - t_0).$$

The velocity-function of the object is $D(t \longmapsto x)$.

In the above expression, a, b, x_0 and t_0 are all fixed numbers (constants).

To find the velocity, we must find

$$D(t \longmapsto a \sin b(t - t_0)).$$

Let $g : t \longmapsto b(t - t_0)$, so that $g' : t \longmapsto b$ and $f = \sin$, so that $f' = \cos$. Then

$$(f \circ g)' = (t \longmapsto \sin b(t - t_0))'$$

Now

$$[(f' \circ g) \times g'](t) = \cos b(t - t_0) \times b$$
$$= b \cos b(t - t_0).$$

It follows that

$$D(t \longmapsto \sin b(t - t_0)) = t \longmapsto b \cos b(t - t_0),$$

and hence that

$$D(t \longmapsto a \sin b(t - t_0)) = t \longmapsto ab \cos b(t - t_0),$$

so the velocity at time t is $ab \cos b(t - t_0)$.

Similarly the acceleration function is $D^2(t \longmapsto x)$; so the acceleration at time t is $-b^2 a \sin b(t - t_0)$. The function (position) $\longmapsto$ (acceleration) is therefore

$$x \longmapsto -b^2 a \sin b(t - t_0),$$

or substituting for t from the formula for position:

$$x \longmapsto -b^2(x - x_0) \quad (x \in R). \qquad \blacksquare$$

12.3.2   Exponential and Logarithmic Functions

Denoting the derived function of the exponential function by $\exp'$, we have from the definition of a derivative:

$$\exp'(x) = \lim_{h \to 0} \frac{\exp(x + h) - \exp(x)}{h} \quad (x \in R)$$

$$= \lim_{h \to 0} \frac{e^{x+h} - e^x}{h} \quad \text{by the exponential theorem (see } Unit \ 7,$$
$$Sequences \ and \ Limits \ I)$$

$$= \lim_{h \to 0} \frac{e^x(e^h - 1)}{h}$$

$$= Ce^x$$

$$= C \exp x$$

where C denotes

$$\lim_{h \to 0} \frac{e^h - 1}{h}.$$

It is shown in Appendix III that this limit exists and $C = 1$, and hence

$$\exp' = \exp. \qquad \qquad \text{Equation (1)}$$

Thus the derived function of exp is the exponential function itself.

This is a remarkable result, but it is no more than might be expected from our introduction to the exponential function via the population growth example which was used in *Unit 7, Sequences and Limits I*. In the model used there, the change in the world's population in a given interval of time was assumed to be proportional to the population itself.

Since differentiation gives the instantaneous rate of change, it is perhaps not so surprising that in differentiating exp we find that the derivative equals exp; we are, after all, considering a quantity (the world's population) whose instantaneous rate of change was (apart from a constant of proportionality) equal to the quantity itself.

The exponential function crops up frequently in applied mathematics because applied mathematics problems (such as the population growth problem) frequently require a function whose derived functions are related to the function itself in a way that can be reduced to Equation (1) by suitable manipulations.

Exercise 1

Use the rule for differentiating inverse functions to show that

$$\ln': x \longmapsto \frac{1}{x} \quad (x \in R^+).$$ ∎

Exercise 1
(3 minutes)

Exercise 2

Show that, for any real function f, with codomain R^+,

$$(\ln \circ f)' = \frac{f'}{f}.$$ ∎

Exercise 2
(3 minutes)

Exercise 3

A useful technique, called logarithmic differentiation, for differentiating a complicated product, f, is to form the composite function, $\ln \circ f$, find its derivative and then obtain f' by using the result in Exercise 2.

(i) Apply this method to the function

$$x \longmapsto e^x \frac{(1+x)}{1+2x} \quad (x \in R \text{ and } x \neq -\tfrac{1}{2}).$$

(ii) Use this method to differentiate $x \longmapsto x^\alpha$ $(x \in R^+)$, where α is any real number. ∎

Exercise 3
(5 minutes)
Definition 1

Solution 1

Solution 1

Since ln is the inverse function of exp, the inverse function rule gives

$$\ln'(x) = \frac{1}{\exp'(\ln x)} = \frac{1}{\exp(\ln x)} = \frac{1}{x} \quad (x \in R^+).$$ ■

Solution 2

Solution 2

The composite function rule gives

$$(\ln \circ f)' = (\ln' \circ f) \times f' = \frac{f'}{f}.$$ ■

Solution 3

Solution 3

(i) Let

$$f(x) = e^x \left(\frac{1+x}{1+2x} \right);$$

then

$$\ln f(x) = x + \ln(1+x) - \ln(1+2x)$$

$$\therefore \frac{f'(x)}{f(x)} = 1 + \frac{1}{1+x} - \frac{2}{1+2x} \quad \text{on differentiating}$$

$$\therefore f'(x) = f(x)\left(1 + \frac{1}{1+x} - \frac{2}{1+2x} \right)$$

$$= e^x \left(\frac{1+x}{1+2x} \right)\left(1 + \frac{1}{1+x} - \frac{2}{1+2x} \right).$$

(ii) Let

$$f : x \longmapsto x^\alpha \quad (x \in R^+)$$

$$f(x) = x^\alpha$$

$$\ln f(x) = \ln(x^\alpha) = \alpha \ln x.$$

Differentiating gives

$$\frac{f'(x)}{f(x)} = \alpha \frac{1}{x}$$

$$f'(x) = \alpha \frac{1}{x} f(x) = \frac{\alpha}{x} x^\alpha = \alpha x^{\alpha - 1}$$

i.e.

$$f' : x \longmapsto \alpha x^{\alpha - 1} \quad (x \in R^+).$$ * * *

We have therefore shown that the function

$$f : x \longmapsto x^\alpha \qquad (x \in R^+)$$

has derived function

$$f' : x \longmapsto \alpha x^{\alpha - 1} \quad (x \in R^+)$$

where α is any real number. ■

12.3.3   Technique of Differentiation

This section is devoted to some exercises to help you learn to apply the rules of differentiation. If you get into difficulties with any of them do not spend a lot of time on it, but look up the solution and compare it with your own attempt, to see where you went wrong. The results of some of these exercises will be useful in *Unit 15, Differentiation II*. There is nothing essentially new in this section, so if you are pressed for time you can leave it for the time being.

Exercise 1

Differentiate:

(i) $f: x \longmapsto x + \dfrac{1}{x}$ $\qquad (x \in R^+);$

(ii) $f: x \longmapsto x \exp(-x)$ $\quad (x \in R);$

(iii) $f: x \longmapsto \dfrac{(x-3)^3}{(x-2)^4}$ $\qquad (x \in R \wedge x > 3).$ ■

Exercise 2

(i) If

$$S: r \longmapsto 2\pi \left(r^2 + \frac{1000}{r\pi} \right) \quad (r \in R^+)$$

find $S'(r)$.

(ii) If

$$f: x \longmapsto \sqrt{x^2 + y^2} \quad (x \in R)$$

where y is some real number (not zero), find f'.

(iii) If

$$P(x) = (x-1)^2 \times (x+2)^2$$

defines the function P with domain R, find $P'(x)$. ■

Exercise 3

Differentiate the function t defined by

$$t(\theta) = \frac{2d}{v_1} \sec \theta + \frac{s - 2d \tan \theta}{v_2} \cdot \left(\theta \in \left[0, \frac{\pi}{2} \right[\right)$$

where d, s, v_1, and v_2 are positive real numbers. ■

Solution 1 **Solution 1**

(i) Standard derived functions give

$$(x \longmapsto x)' = (x \longmapsto 1),$$

and

$$(x \longmapsto x^{-1})' = (x \longmapsto -x^{-2});$$

it follows by the addition rule that

$$\left(x \longmapsto x + \frac{1}{x}\right)' = \left(x \longmapsto 1 - \frac{1}{x^2}\right) \qquad (x \in R^+).$$

(ii) The given function has the product form

$$f = gh$$

where

$$g(x) = x \qquad (x \in R)$$
$$h(x) = \exp(-x) \quad (x \in R).$$

Moreover, $h(x)$ is of the form $\exp(k(x))$ where

$$k(x) = -x \qquad (x \in R).$$

By the "function of a function" rule, the derived function of h is given by

$$h'(x) = \exp'(k(x)) \times k'(x) = \exp(-x)(-1)$$
$$= -\exp(-x).$$

By the product rule, the derived function of f is therefore given by:

$$f'(x) = g'(x)h(x) + g(x)h'(x)$$
$$= 1 \exp(-x) + x(-\exp(-x))$$
$$= (1 - x)\exp(-x) \qquad (x \in R).$$

(iii) We could differentiate directly using the quotient rule, but it is easier to use logarithmic differentiation (see Exercise 12.3.2.3). That is, we write down the formula for $f(x)$ as usual

$$f(x) = \frac{(x-3)^3}{(x-2)^4}$$

but before differentiating we take natural logarithms, obtaining

$$\ln f(x) = 3 \ln(x-3) - 4 \ln(x-2)$$

and then, by the "function of a function" rule,

$$\ln'(f(x))f'(x) = 3 \ln'(x-3) - 4 \ln'(x-2)$$

(since $(x \longmapsto x - 3)' = x \longmapsto 1$ and $(x \longmapsto x - 2)' = x \longmapsto 1$).

Since $\ln'(u) = \frac{1}{u}$, this simplifies to

$$\frac{f'(x)}{f(x)} = \frac{3}{x-3} - \frac{4}{x-2}$$

so that

$$f'(x) = \left(\frac{3}{x-3} - \frac{4}{x-2}\right) f(x)$$
$$= \left(\frac{3}{x-3} - \frac{4}{x-2}\right) \frac{(x-3)^3}{(x-2)^4} \qquad (x \in R \land x > 3). \quad \blacksquare$$

Solution 2

Solution 2

(i)
$$S(r) = 2\pi\left(r^2 + \frac{1000}{\pi r}\right).$$

Standard derived functions and the rule for constant factors give

$$(r \longmapsto r^2)' = (r \longmapsto 2r),$$

and

$$\left(r \longmapsto \frac{1000}{\pi} r^{-1}\right)' = \left(r \longmapsto -\frac{1000}{\pi} r^{-2}\right),$$

therefore the addition rule and the rule for multiplication by a constant give

$$S'(r) = 2\pi\left(2r - \frac{1000}{\pi r^2}\right).$$

(ii) The function can be expressed as a composition:

$$f(x) = g(h(x))$$

where

$$h(x) = x^2 + y^2 \quad (x \in R)$$

and

$$g(u) = \sqrt{u} \qquad (u \in R^+).$$

The derived functions of h and g are such that

$$h'(x) = 2x + 0 \quad \text{(by the sum rule)}$$

$$g'(u) = \tfrac{1}{2} u^{-1/2} = \frac{1}{2\sqrt{u}}.$$

The rule for differentiating composite functions gives

$$f'(x) = g'(h(x)) \times h'(x)$$

$$= \frac{1}{2\sqrt{h(x)}} \times 2x$$

$$= \frac{x}{\sqrt{x^2 + y^2}}$$

and so the answer to 'the exercise is

$$f' : x \longmapsto \frac{x}{\sqrt{x^2 + y^2}} \quad (x \in R).$$

(Since y is not zero, the denominator of $f'(x)$ is never zero.)

(iii) The given function is of the form

$$P = QS$$

with

$$Q(x) = (x - 1)^2 \quad (x \in R)$$

$$S(x) = (x + 2)^2 \quad (x \in R).$$

These functions are compositions; for example

$$Q = F \circ G$$

where

$$F(u) = u^2 \qquad (u \in R)$$

$$G(x) = x - 1 \qquad (x \in R).$$

The rule for differentiating composite functions gives

$$Q'(x) = F'(G(x)) \times G'(x)$$
$$= 2G(x) \times 1$$
$$= 2(x - 1).$$

Similarly, we have

$$S'(x) = 2(x + 2).$$

The product rule therefore gives

$$P'(x) = Q'(x)S(x) + Q(x)S'(x)$$
$$= 2(x - 1)(x + 2)^2 + (x - 1)^2 2(x + 2)$$
$$= 2(x - 1)(x + 2)(2x + 1). \qquad \blacksquare$$

Solution 3

We know from our list of standard forms that

$$\sec' \theta = \sec \theta \tan \theta$$

and

$$\tan' \theta = \sec^2 \theta.$$

It follows that

$$t'(\theta) = \frac{2d}{v_1} \sec \theta \tan \theta + \frac{-2d \sec^2 \theta}{v_2}$$

which defines t', since the domain is already given as $\left[0, \dfrac{\pi}{2} \right[$. $\qquad \blacksquare$

12.4   SUMMARIES

12.4.0   Summary of Unit

We began the unit with revision of the idea of average rate of change. We considered distance and the average rate of change of distance, which we called the average velocity. The average velocity was shown to be inadequate as a measure of the instantaneous velocity, and a difficulty in this last definition was overcome by means of a limit process. We thus arrived at the definition of the derivative of a function at an element in its domain, and this was generalized to obtain the derived function. In the rest of the unit we developed techniques for differentiation. We obtained rules for differentiation of functions in the forms:

$$f + g, f \times g, \frac{f}{g}, f \circ g, \text{ and the inverse of a one–one function } f.$$

We then applied these rules to polynomial, trigonometric, exponential and logarithmic functions.

12.4.1 Summary of Rules and Formulas for Differentiation

Rules for differentiation

1 If $g = af$, then $g' = af'$.

2 If $h = f + g$, then $h' = f' + g'$ (sum rule).

3 If $h = fg$, then $h' = f'g + fg'$ (product rule).

4 If $h = \dfrac{f}{g}$, then $h' = \dfrac{f'g - fg'}{g^2}$ (quotient rule).

5 If $h = f \circ g$, then $h' = (f' \circ g) \times g'$ (composite function rule).

6 If f is one–one and g is the inverse of f, then $f' = \dfrac{1}{g' \circ f}$.

Standard derived functions

f	f'	Domain of f'	Remarks
$x \longmapsto x^m$	$x \longmapsto mx^{m-1}$	R	$m \in Z^+$
$x \longmapsto x^m$	$x \longmapsto mx^{m-1}$	R without 0	$m \in Z$
$x \longmapsto x^m$	$x \longmapsto mx^{m-1}$	R^+	$m \in R$
$x \longmapsto \exp x$	$x \longmapsto \exp x$	R	
$x \longmapsto \ln x$	$x \longmapsto \dfrac{1}{x}$	R^+	
$x \longmapsto \sin x$	$x \longmapsto \cos x$	R	
$x \longmapsto \cos x$	$x \longmapsto -\sin x$	R	

Some further derived functions (obtainable from the above)

f	f'	Domain of f'
$x \longmapsto \tan x$	$x \longmapsto \sec^2 x$	R excluding $\pm\dfrac{\pi}{2}, \pm\dfrac{3\pi}{2}, \ldots$
$x \longmapsto \sec x$	$x \longmapsto \sec x \tan x$	R excluding $\pm\dfrac{\pi}{2}, \pm\dfrac{3\pi}{2}, \ldots$
$x \longmapsto \cot x$	$x \longmapsto \csc^2 x$	R excluding $0, \pm\pi, \pm 2\pi, \ldots$
$x \longmapsto \csc x$	$x \longmapsto -\csc x \cot x$	R excluding $0, \pm\pi, \pm 2\pi, \ldots$

12.5   APPENDICES (Not part of the course)

12.5.1   Appendix I: The Leibniz Notation

Probably the most widely used notation for calculus is the one invented by Leibniz. In this notation, if x is a variable representing an element in the domain of a function, f, and y is another variable whose value is related to that of x by

$$y = f(x) \qquad (x \in \text{domain of } f),$$

then we use the symbol $\dfrac{dy}{dx}$ to stand for $f'(x)$. That is, we define

$$\frac{dy}{dx} = f'(x) \quad (x \in \text{domain of } f').$$

The advantage of the Leibniz notation is its conciseness; for example, the formula giving the derived function of $x \longmapsto x^2$ $(x \in R)$ can be written

$$\frac{d(x^2)}{dx} = 2x$$

instead of

$$(x \longmapsto x^2)' = (x \longmapsto 2x).$$

The process of calculating $\dfrac{dy}{dx}$, when y is defined as an expression involving x (for example the x^2 in the above example), is called *differentiating* this expression *with respect to x*. Formally, we may say that to differentiate y with respect to x is to calculate $f'(x)$ where f is the function defined by

$$f : x \longmapsto y.$$

The disadvantage of the Leibniz notation is that it contains some traps for the beginner, arising from the difficulty of assigning an independent meaning to the symbols dx and dy when they occur separately (rather than locked together in the combination $\dfrac{dy}{dx}$). Since the principles of calculus can be understood without using Leibniz notation, it is not treated as an essential part of this Foundation Course.

Thus the rules for differentiating sums and products in the Leibniz notation become

$$\frac{d(u + v)}{dx} = \frac{du}{dx} + \frac{dv}{dx},$$

$$\frac{d(cu)}{dx} = c\frac{du}{dx} \text{ if } c \text{ is a constant}$$

(i.e. if $x \longmapsto c$ is a constant function),

$$\frac{d(uv)}{dx} = u\frac{dv}{dx} + v\frac{du}{dx}.$$

To express the rule for differentiating composite functions in this notation, let x, y and z be variables related by

$$y = g(x) \qquad\qquad (x \in \text{domain of } g)$$

$$z = f(y) \qquad\qquad (y \in \text{domain of } f)$$

so that

$$g'(x) = \frac{dy}{dx} \qquad\qquad (x \in \text{domain of } g'),$$

$$f'(g(x)) = f'(y) = \frac{dz}{dy} \quad (y \in \text{domain of } f'),$$

Then the rule for differentiating a function h defined by

$$h(x) = f(g(x)) \qquad (x \in \text{domain of } h)$$

is

$$h'(x) = f'(g(x)) \times g'(x) \quad (x \in \text{domain of } h')$$

which takes the simple form

$$\frac{dz}{dx} = \frac{dz}{dy} \times \frac{dy}{dx}.$$

This rule is called the chain rule and is easy to remember because one can think of dy as "cancelling out" from the expression on the right.

The rule for differentiating inverse functions also takes a convenient form in this notation: it is

$$\frac{dy}{dx} = \frac{1}{\left(\dfrac{dx}{dy}\right)}.$$

The proof is similar to the proof of the chain rule. We shall not go into details here.

There is a very good discussion of the Leibniz notation on page 171 of T. M. Apostol, *Calculus* (see Bibliography).

12.5.2 Appendix II: Differentiation of sin and cos

To differentiate sin we use the definition of a derivative, obtaining

$$\sin'(x) = \lim_{h \to 0} \left(\frac{\sin(x + h) - \sin x}{h} \right)$$

$$= \lim_{h \to 0} \left(\frac{\sin x \cos h}{h} + \frac{\cos x \sin h}{h} - \frac{\sin x}{h} \right).$$

Collecting together the parts that are proportional to $\cos x$ and $\sin x$, we have:

$$\sin'(x) = \cos x \lim_{h \to 0} \frac{\sin h}{h} + \sin x \lim_{h \to 0} \frac{\cos h - 1}{h} \qquad \text{Equation (1)}$$

(since $\cos x$ and $\sin x$ are independent of h). The evaluation of the limit of $\dfrac{\sin h}{h}$ at 0 can be demonstrated on the diagram:

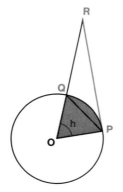

57

The arc PQ subtends an angle h radians at the centre O of the circle, which has unit radius. PR is a tangent and OQR is a straight line. In this diagram there are three areas that can be simply expressed in terms of the angle h and its trigonometric functions:

$$\text{triangle } OPR = \tfrac{1}{2} \times \text{base} \times \text{height} = \tfrac{1}{2} OP \times PR$$

$$= \tfrac{1}{2} OP \times OP \tan h = \tfrac{1}{2} \tan h$$

$$\text{shaded sector } OPQ = \frac{h}{2\pi} \times \text{area of circle}$$

$$= \frac{h}{2\pi} \times \pi OP^2 = \tfrac{1}{2} h$$

$$\text{triangle } OPQ = \tfrac{1}{2} \text{base} \times \text{height}$$

$$= \tfrac{1}{2} OP \times OQ \sin h = \tfrac{1}{2} \sin h.$$

Geometrical intuition tells us that $\left(\text{if } 0 < h < \dfrac{\pi}{2} \right)$

$$\text{triangle } OPQ < \text{sector } OPQ, \text{ i.e. } \tfrac{1}{2} \sin h < \tfrac{1}{2} h$$

and

$$\text{sector } OPQ < \text{triangle } OPR, \text{ i.e. } \tfrac{1}{2} h < \tfrac{1}{2} \tan h.$$

The fact that we are relying on geometrical intuition here means that the result of this appendix is demonstrated, not proven, after all, the definition of sin that we are using is itself geometrical. The whole argument, including the definition of the trigonometric functions, can be made rigorous without any reliance on geometrical intuition.

Since we are assuming $h > 0$, we may multiply both sides of the inequality $\tfrac{1}{2} \sin h < \tfrac{1}{2} h$ by $\dfrac{2}{h}$, and since we are assuming $h < \dfrac{\pi}{2}$, which (with $h > 0$) implies $\cos h > 0$, we may multiply both sides of the inequality $\tfrac{1}{2} h < \tfrac{1}{2} \tan h$ by $\dfrac{2 \cos h}{h}$. Combining the two resulting inequalities we obtain:

$$\cos h < \frac{\sin h}{h} < 1 \quad \left(0 < h < \frac{\pi}{2} \right).$$

(For the rules for the manipulation of inequalities see *Unit 6, Inequalities*.) Since both $\cos h$ and $\dfrac{\sin h}{h}$ stay the same when the sign of h is changed, these inequalities imply

$$\cos h < \frac{\sin h}{h} < 1 \quad \left(-\frac{\pi}{2} < h < 0 \right).$$

We know from the geometrical definition of $\cos h$ that we can make $\cos h$ as close to 1 as we please by making h small enough, i.e. that

$$\lim_{h \to 0} \cos h = 1.$$

When $|h|$ is very small, therefore, the value of $\dfrac{\sin h}{h}$ is sandwiched in between 1 and a number whose limit is 1. It follows that $\dfrac{\sin h}{h}$ must also have the limit 1 near 0:

$$\lim_{h \to 0} \frac{\sin h}{h} = 1 \qquad \text{Equation (2)}$$

To evaluate the other limit in Equation (1) we reduce it to the preceding one, obtaining

$$\lim_{h \to 0} \frac{\cos h - 1}{h} = \lim_{h \to 0} \frac{2 \sin^2 \frac{1}{2}h}{h}$$

(See RB10)

$$= \lim_{h \to 0} \frac{h}{2} \times \left(\frac{\sin \frac{1}{2}h}{\frac{1}{2}h} \right)^2$$

$$= \lim_{h \to 0} \frac{h}{2} \times \left(\lim_{h \to 0} \frac{\sin \frac{1}{2}h}{\frac{1}{2}h} \right)^2$$

$$= 0 \times 1^2 = 0,$$

Equation (3)

since $\lim_{h \to 0}$ and $\lim_{(1/2)h \to 0}$ are the same, by the definition of a limit. From Equations (2) and (3) in Equation (1), we have

$$\sin'(x) = \cos x \quad (x \in R).$$

12.5.3 Appendix III: Evaluation of $\lim_{h \to 0} \dfrac{e^h - 1}{h}$

We use the definition of exp given in Section 7.4.1 of *Unit 7, Sequences and Limits I*, obtaining

$$\frac{e^h - 1}{h} = \lim_{n \text{ large}} \left\{ \frac{\left(1 + \dfrac{h}{n} \right)^n - 1}{h} \right\}$$

$$= \lim_{n \text{ large}} \left\{ \frac{h + \dfrac{h^2}{2} \times \dfrac{n-1}{n} + \cdots + \dfrac{h^n}{n^n}}{h} \right\}$$

Equation (1)

by the binomial theorem. If $h > 0$, the numerator satisfies

$$h \leqslant \text{numerator} \leqslant h + \frac{h^2}{2} + \cdots + \frac{h^n}{n^n}$$

$$\leqslant h + h^2 + \cdots + h^n$$

$$= h \frac{1 - h^n}{1 - h} \leqslant \frac{h}{1 - h} \quad \text{provided } h < 1.$$

(See RB8)

On using these inequalities in Equation (1), we find that

$$1 \leqslant \frac{e^h - 1}{h} \leqslant \frac{1}{1 - h} \quad \text{when } 0 < h < 1.$$

If $h < 0$, a similar method shows that

$$1 \geqslant \frac{e^h - 1}{h} \geqslant 1 - \frac{h}{1 - h}.$$

Now we know that $\lim_{h \to 0} \dfrac{1}{1 - h} = 1$ and that $\lim_{h \to 0} 1 - \dfrac{h}{1 - h} = 1$. Thus, whether h is positive or negative, when it is very small the value of $\dfrac{e^h - 1}{h}$ must be very close to 1, and we conclude that

$$\lim_{h \to 0} \frac{e^h - 1}{h} = 1.$$

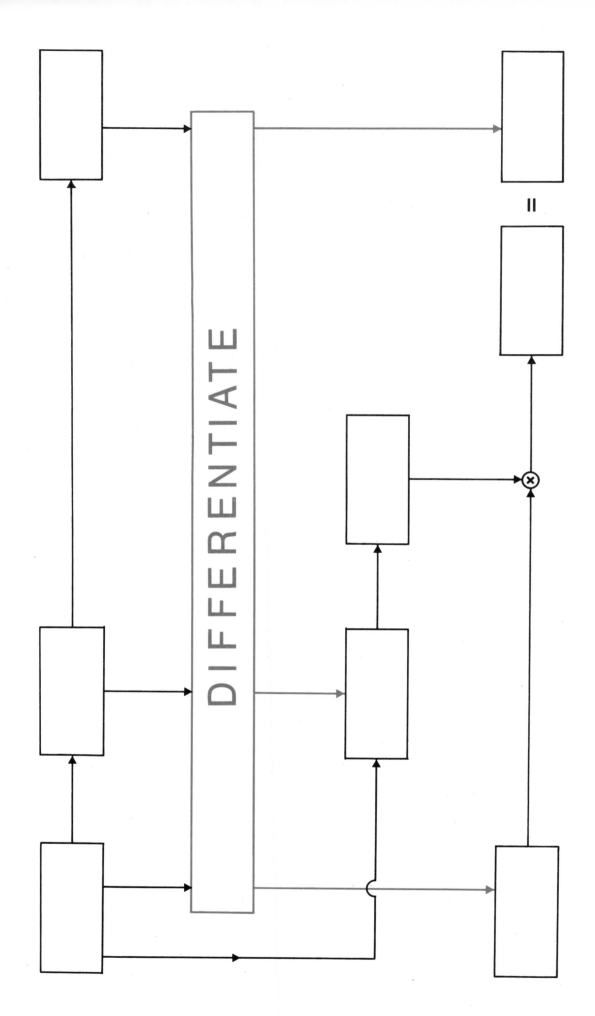

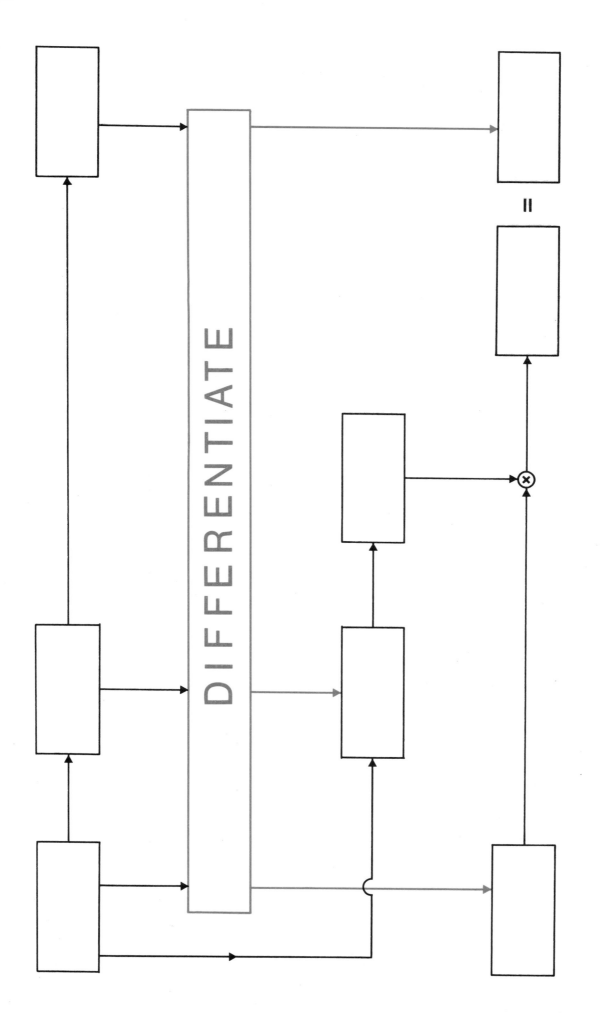

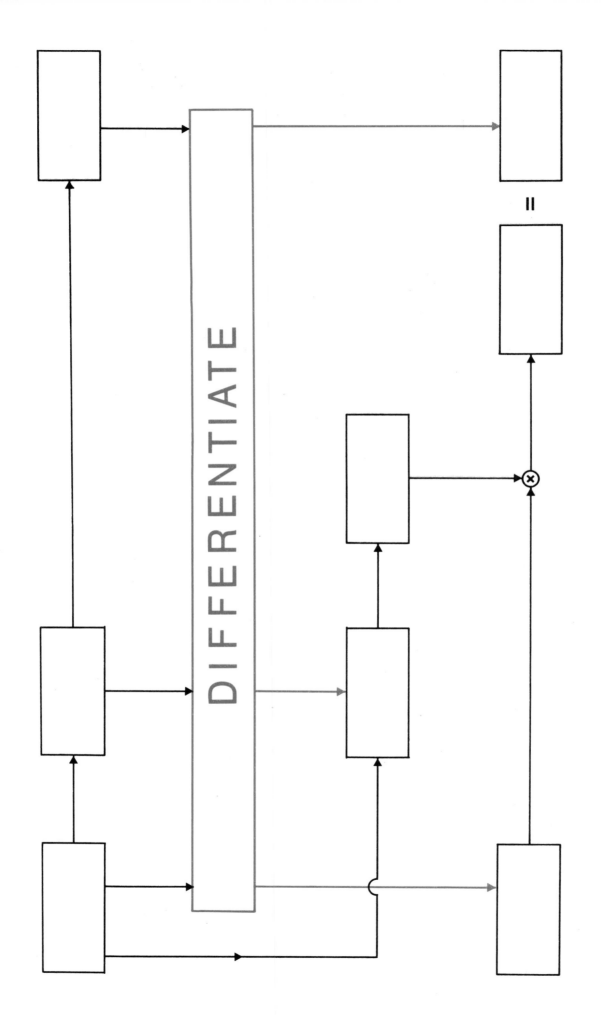

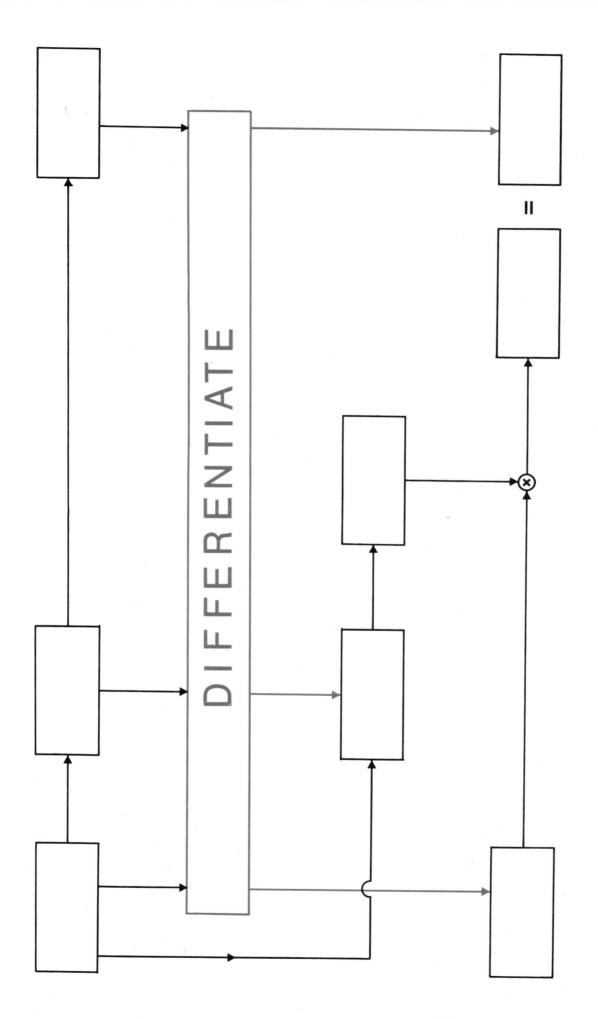

Unit No.		Title of Text
1		Functions
2		Errors and Accuracy
3		Operations and Morphisms
4		Finite Differences
5	NO TEXT	
6		Inequalities
7		Sequences and Limits I
8		Computing I
9		Integration I
10	NO TEXT	
11		Logic I — Boolean Algebra
12		Differentiation I
13		Integration II
14		Sequences and Limits II
15		Differentiation II
16		Probability and Statistics I
17		Logic II — Proof
18		Probability and Statistics II
19		Relations
20		Computing II
21		Probability and Statistics III
22		Linear Algebra I
23		Linear Algebra II
24		Differential Equations I
25	NO TEXT	
26		Linear Algebra III
27		Complex Numbers I
28		Linear Algebra IV
29		Complex Numbers II
30		Groups I
31		Differential Equations II
32	NO TEXT	
33		Groups II
34		Number Systems
35		Topology
36		Mathematical Structures